What **NOT** to eat in a **Restaurant**

A light-hearted Guide to Avoiding Dodgy
Food When Eating at a Restaurant

CARRIE HERRING

Dedicated to…

All the good, clean restaurants and staff that this book does not apply to.

Acknowledgments

Thanks to all the great leaders in my life whose words are permanently ingrained in my head. From my first boss, who said, "Never ever put your fingers in a glass, even if you're in a room alone," to one of my latest managers, who said, "You're only as good as your last game."

Note from the Author

This note is to reiterate that I am not trying to single out any restaurant or type of restaurant. Mistakes can happen anywhere, across the board! In over 30 years of service, I don't think I have ever seen any vicious, intentional behavior—things just get overlooked. Most servers, hosts, bartenders, cooks, chefs, bussers, owners, managers, and dishwashers take pride in themselves and their work.

No one is out to get you, so do not think for one minute that this is one of "those" books. Even after being verbally abused and insulted, servers will almost never take it out on your food.

Contents

INTRODUCTION:
EAT AT YOUR OWN RISK!

The food business is a strange place, where a lot of weird things happen. It is not surprising however; after all, it is one of the most demanding service sectors in the world—with fierce standards, lots of different people, and customers that insist on the best.

In a lot of ways, that makes the restaurant biz a playground for common mistakes, overlooked concerns, and hilarious staff blunders. Service staff never intentionally mean to serve gross things to their customers, but it happens more often than anyone wants to admit! Restaurants are a constant source of inspiration for me because the challenge never ends.

This book is a result of many solid years in the restaurant industry, working with a variety of folks and handling a host of sticky situations. I have been a waitress and a bartender and have seen my fair share of things that would make the average person just a little more cautious about where they eat and what they choose off a menu.

If you love to eat out or you work in a restaurant every day, I want to invite you to come along with me on this journey. It is a journey into the heart of an industry that thrives on good intentions and yet is still hampered by the little mistakes we all make. These little mistakes add up over time, resulting in some pretty wayward stuff!

I want to give you a glimpse of this world so that you can appreciate the inner workings of a restaurant and bar and can make your own decisions based on this insider knowledge. Once you know what happens in a restaurant, you can never un-know it.

That is why I want to share these stories with you. Wherever you go, you need to be aware that you eat there at your own risk! The choices you make about where you eat and what you eat are important—especially if you have a habit of running into food poisoning fairly often. This guide will help you make better decisions about the secret restaurant industry.

Think of this fun little guide as your shield against the pandemonium that can and does break out sometimes, even in the best of restaurants. There are things you should know, my friends, and these things could save your life! Well, they could save you a night of food poisoning anyway. And no one wants to cross that bridge by mistake.

Join me on a romp through where, when, and how you should eat out at your local restaurants. This is the guide few restaurant owners would publish. It is a veritable tome of information regarding the dodgy practices that exist in our wonderful food industry today. Sit back, kick up your feet, and enjoy.

You will never eat out the same way again.

Where To Never Eat And Why

CHAPTER 1
THE DODGY DINING LIST

> *"As a restaurateur, my job is to basically control the chaos and the drama. There's always going to be chaos in the restaurant business."*
>
> — ROCCO DISPIRITO

Navigating the sometimes overcrowded, understaffed, and poorly managed restaurants of the world can be a challenge, even for seasoned travelers and local foodies. During my 30-year career, I have worked in dozens of restaurants, unearthing hidden gems about the industry that you should know about.

In this chapter, I want to share with you where you should never eat and why. The term "never" is open to interpretation of course. When I say I "never" go somewhere, I do not until I do—and then I make sure that I only order what I know to be clean, safe, and idiot-proof. Here is your very lenient dodgy dining list to help you whisk yourself to the right local places.

Family-Owned Mom & Pop Restaurants

A mom and pop restaurant is usually a small, independent, family-owned business. They are not franchises and large corporations, and because of this, they tend to be a little more prone to folly than their larger counterparts.

Inexperience is really the enemy of these family-owned restaurants. They might have the best food in town because of a passionate chef–owner, but hidden in the floury shadows are ill-developed operational procedures that are left up to their 15-year-old server, who is also suffering from teen angst and boyfriend trouble.

These mom and pop restaurants are usually great in some areas and woefully lacking in others. It makes sense—the owner has to feel their way through the day, changing and improving things as he or she goes. It is ridiculous to believe that every restaurant owner is well trained and more than equipped to handle a few hundred diners each day.

So my warning for these often fine establishments is this: Be aware that cutlery might not be clean all the time due to shoddy washing procedures. Be aware[1] that they may be short staffed or underfunded, so being aware of good menu selections is important. Most of all, be aware that they are doing the best they can, but they will be far from perfect.

Support their food, but do not abort your responsibilities! Take note of your environmental surroundings, the hygiene of the place, and the quality of the people. Their goal is to make success happen, but success is a rocky road littered with operational mistakes.

Recipes may not be done correctly (people with allergies, watch out!), customer service could be lacking, and roles may not be clearly defined. Try not to order the weirdest thing on the menu!

---

1   David S. Peters, *Top 5 Mistakes of Mom and Pop Restaurants*, http://therestaurantexpert.com/top-5-mistakes-of-mom-and-pop-restaurants/

The Franchise Reality

Ah yes, the noble franchise! You may know these restaurants as the beloved food chains and fast food restaurants that you grew up with. Franchises in the restaurant industry are restaurants that license out their business model to investors that want to mimic the operational success of the original model. This comes with a well-known brand and a built-in community.

Highly competitive industries like fast food have the most franchises. These are super-powered, super-fast, and ultra-tight businesses that are honed by strategic experts and operational wizards so that the machine runs like clockwork and produces consistency—no matter where the branch may be or which team is running it.

The good news is that franchise food operations are usually so good that it is nearly impossible to get food poisoning from this kind of food. Improbable, not impossible, is probably more accurate. As you already know, when things do go wrong, they tend to go wrong in a big way, and the news teams get involved.

The reality of franchises is the same as any other restaurant, if you consider how many franchises open and close their doors each year. A new franchisee is prone to the same mistakes (and a lot more stress) than mom and pop stores when they open. Along with having a financial investment in their own company, they also have to follow a huge set of rules.

This leads to starter franchisees'[2] making a lot of mistakes when they open their doors. Their staff turnover may be high, so they may be in a constant state of training, hiring, and firing. This can lead to the incorrect implementation of operational procedures. Then there is the food itself. Often large chains are about the bottom line—the money!

---

2   *Karsten Strauss, 13 Mistakes New Franchisees Make—And How to Avoid Them, http://www.forbes.com/sites/karstenstrauss/2014/05/27/13-mistakes-new-franchisees-make-and-how-to-avoid-them/*

This means that they may resort to unhealthy or incorrect food practices to make money, as was famously exposed in many McDonalds and KFC scandals over the years with "chemical beef" and "mutated chicken." This is always something to watch out for when eating at a franchise. Then there are some lesser known concerns.

It helps, for example, to get to know the food practices of your favorite local franchise. A specific dish on the menu may be prepared in the worst way possible, according to the staff. You just will not know until you ask. On Reddit recently, an employee at a famous franchise revealed never to eat the fish because it was always cooked in month-old black oil.

Pizza is a safe bet for a franchise, but watch out for the characteristic "thumb print" in the pizza base to check if it has been cooked thoroughly. A dirty thumb in the pizza crust is the most unhygienic part of the pizza.

The Country Club Myth

Who can withstand the allure of a nice country club lunch? Traditionally, a country club is a private member club with a host of lovely sporting and social facilities set in an idyllic rural setting of rolling hills and flowing lakes. On first impression, you could not imagine that anything could possibly go wrong with such an upmarket establishment.

But things do go wrong, and they go wrong often! When I worked over at a country club, I was always flabbergasted that no one complained of cold food. The staff, impressed by their own brilliance and creativity, would spend several long, drawn out minutes plating the food in layers, culminating in a fingerprint-laden, cold dish for the customer.

I guess the down side to enjoying something expensive and unusual is that it takes a long time to plate, with an overly complicated stacking process. First the grains would be placed on the plate then carrots that had to face to the south. Then an herbed butter patty would go on top of the main meat in the dish, followed by a demi glaze.

After that there was still the festooning of parsley on the plate, along with the cleaning process to wipe all excess fingerprints away. Playing with this food stack means that every part of your food has been touched thoroughly by multiple people.

While country clubs are excellent at finding the best quality products and they pay solid wages and drug test so their staff tend to be great—you are still not 100% safe. Waiters sometimes pull a guest's dirty napkin out of the laundry to wipe down another guests plate or an entire table's silverware.

I know of one country club, lavish as it was, that stayed open and kept serving despite a water ban where sewerage had leaked into their water supply. In my opinion, all the food that came into contact with that water was contaminated—but it was not enough to "disappoint" the guests and turn them away. I think if they had known, they would have willingly left.

So even expensive country clubs that focus on the finer things have their troubles.[3] While the food may always be fresh and prepared in a creative way, you are not immune to staff fingers, misconduct, or "cutting corners." After a hard day's work or a double shift, you just never know what a tired server or barperson will do to conserve energy.

My advice would be to order something simple that does not have so many complex layers—even though these can be tempting. The less your food is handled by people, the less likely it is to carry bacteria that will make you ill. And always clean off your utensils yourself before indulging in a meal; they may have been smeared with someone else's germs!

---

3 Amy Davis, *Restaurant Report Card: Country Club Has Hygiene Issue, http:// www.click2houston.com/news/money/restaurant-report-card-country-club-has-hygiene-issue/28020056*

A Bar by Any Other Name

Few things are as fun as heading down to your local bar and having a drink with a friend and a casual bite to eat. Bars may not be popular for their food, but even the ones that are can have some questionable practices. I have worked in many bars during my career, and I know all of the tricks of the trade.

Harmless bar snacks are never that harmless. I have marveled at customers eating from bowls of nuts and snacks that do not even bother to hide the fact that they lick their fingers and contaminate the rest of the food for everyone else! You cannot blame that on the staff, but at the same time, you cannot remove the complimentary nuts either. It is your choice to eat them.

Then there are the questionable hygiene practices in bars that are brought about by drunkenness and a lack of operational proficiency. Bars are privately owned, which means that resources can be spread too thin.

It is not uncommon for bar staff to be hired on a shoestring budget, which does not always attract the best quality of employee. Best case scenario you get youngsters that are still studying and need "extra" cash; worst case scenario you get adults with real problems that need a job just to cover some basics.

For the bars that hire cheap staff, cheap service results. Food is incorrectly stored, labelled, and handled, and this means illness for bar patrons. Then there is all the alcohol, which attracts more than a few pests like roaches and rats. These pests can really degenerate the hygiene of a place, especially when it was not great to begin with.

The dingiest[4] bar is far, far worse that the poorest country club, so my advice would be to never eat open snacks off a table. Do not even drink the table water. Sometimes it stands for ages, and

---

4   *Mistakes To Avoid When Running Your Bar, http://www.entrepreneur.com/ article/232499*

sometimes drunk people drink from it without a glass. The finest bars are clean and have friendly, well-trained staff, and they take care during food preparation and storage.

The staff should not be allowed to drink, even after hours, in order to maintain the integrity of the place. Staff that are allowed to drink will make a lot more mistakes than sober staff. These mistakes may include the types of behavior that rapidly degenerate the hygiene of the establishment by drinking and eating there.

I have seen customers and staff drink directly from a draft beer tap then proceed to pour some fresh ones for other people—gross! It is best to keep it to bottled beer and beverages if you suspect that the place can get a little overly rowdy. As for the food, keep your ordering simple, and stick to the classics that they make often and are known for.

Private Clubs & Catering

Private clubs and catering companies are two more places that each have their own special set of concerns. Again, while some companies excel and are extremely good at what they do, most of these places are privately run, and because of that, they have their own special way of doing things. I have worked in a few of these, and it can vary a lot!

Private clubs like veteran and yacht clubs play by their own set of rules. It is not uncommon to find someone in charge of the kitchen that has never professionally studied to be there and has no idea how to really handle, store, or prepare food for many people. That means a lot of safety falls by the wayside.

Sometimes a member of the club is placed in charge of the restaurant along with a restaurant manager, who is supposed to know how things work. But with a lack of leadership, things can quickly go wrong. I have seen cooks exiting the bathroom with their aprons still on, which would not happen if operational procedures were in place.

Private clubs are like eating at a friend's house; you never know what you are going to get. As one of the most questionable forms of restaurant to eat at, you have to ask the right questions. Who runs the place? Are they qualified? Are they experienced? Is the staff well paid and trained well? If these are not evident, run for the hills!

Many a private club has hired cheap staff that do n0t know how to serve. Along with not getting the food out on time, you are then made to endure a level of service that is uncaring, distant, and confused. Better to save your money and go to the local diner down the street. At least the owners will be there, and they care about the food they serve.

With catering companies,[5] there are always red flags. Food is prepared in one place and moved to another. Or food is created in an unfamiliar kitchen that may not be hygienic at all. Unlicensed catering companies are rife, and problems always arise with poor practices. In fact, more people are food poisoned through catering companies than restaurants.

Thanks to hot food becoming lukewarm and cold food warming up, food poisoning can strike at any time. Improper handling of chicken and leafy green vegetables is a common culprit. You just never know what you are going to get from a catering company, so if the food looks suspicious, do not eat it.

Avoid the chicken dishes and salad bar if you are really concerned. These are the most likely places where salmonella and other bacteria can gather over time. Rather be safe than sorry when eating from either of these distinguished places.

Churches & Local Festivals

The last two food locations that you need to be wary of belong to two large gathering spots—churches and local festivals. Churches

---

5   *Caterers Dish Up More Cases of Food Poisoning, http://www.nbcnews.com/ id/38420815/ns/health-food_safety/t/caterers-dish-more-cases-food-poisoning/#.VX_ zuvmqpBc*

often host fundraisers and food events to get the community together for a special event or a donation drive for a charity.

The trouble comes in when local people are suddenly placed in a position where they have to create food for hundreds of people. Hygiene and safety become compromised because of a lack of culinary training, and this ends up in contaminated food and bouts of food poisoning scattered among the church members.

For some people, a small amount of salmonella is enough to trigger a huge response, while many others will not be impacted by it at all. But it is not uncommon for church food makers to not wear gloves, to never wash their utensils between dishes, to have no hand washing policy, and to serve guests on less than clean plates with poorly-washed implements.

When eating at these food stalls, you need to consider that hygiene is not at the top of their list of priorities. Serving the most people quickly is at the top. That means if a spatula is dropped on the floor, a quick rinse is fine. It means if you get overwhelmed, telling people to help themselves is not uncommon. And this can lead to contamination!

In addition, you have to consider that at some local festivals, the food servers will be less than sober; exhausted from the rush of breakfast, lunch, and supper; and eager to cut corners wherever they can. I have seen festival staff spread pizza sauce with their hands, and I have seen church staff dig food containers out of unhygienic areas.

I always like to consider these locations as the same as eating at a complete stranger's house. You just do not know what you are going to get, so it is best to be mildly suspicious of everything. That way you can make the best decisions possible and avoid buying food that is contaminated with germs.

One thing is for sure: These food creators and servers are most likely untrained and have no idea how to maintain the kind of health and safety standards you can get at a normal restaurant. At least those places have health inspections! Try to find a food truck that has had a health inspection lately, and you will be doing well.

A good place to eat out is at a diner. The menus are small, so the produce is always fresh. The servers are permanent and are paid well, plus they are made up of locals. Locals always know what is best to eat on the menu. These can be dirty, but for the most part, if you have to eat somewhere foreign, a diner should be a safer pick.

CHAPTER 2
RESTAURANT WARNING SIGNS

> *"It all comes back to the basics. Serve customers the best-tasting food at a good value in a clean, comfortable restaurant, and they'll keep coming back."*
>
> DAVE THOMAS

Nearly all restaurants have varying standards of service, hygiene, and discipline when it comes to maintaining operational efficiency. There are some restaurant warning signs that you need to look out for so that you can have a great dining-out experience.

In this chapter, I am going to expose some not-so-brilliant practices that act as clear warning bells when you walk into a new restaurant. Use these to assess how the restaurant operates and whether you should eat there. There is never any shame in getting up and leaving!

Young Workers: Games They Play!

There are a lot of reasons why a restaurant can suffer from poor service. One of the main reasons I have found is that most of the servers are young, and young people love to play pranks and jokes on each other. Along with helping to move your day along, it makes things interesting, is amusing, and is good for team building at the restaurant.

But sometimes these pranks[6] can be a little distracting and can lead to poor service. I knew a team of servers that played pranks on each other all the time when service was slow. At one point, it got out of hand, and a trick backfired on a customer, who was not amused.

Young workers need entertainment, and they like to mess around during the day. Sometimes this means simple things like adding salt in their coffee or tampering with their staff meals. Other times it can mean dying an apron pink. Whatever the prank, whether harmless or not, it can mean issues for the customer.

The most common issue is, of course, *neglect*. You have experienced it before. You walk into a nice restaurant, it is quiet, and the staff is so wrapped up in their own worlds that they do not even see you walk in. As a result, you get poor service for the duration of your stay. Your food is badly prepared, and the staff are overly distracted.

If you walk into a restaurant and it is full of giggling teenagers—or even young students—beware. Chances are, you are not going to get great service. They are not thinking about you; they are thinking about seeking revenge on one of their co-workers for putting an anchovy in their hat yesterday.

While this is not such a huge deal, it can lead to mistakes and bad service. And any restaurant owner will tell you that 50% of an experience is about service.

---

6   *Epic Restaurant Pranks, http://www.johnnaknowsgoodfood.com/2012/04/25/epic-restaurant-pranks/*

Franchises That Do Not Pay Well

One of the biggest issues in the restaurant industry today is that many of them simply do not pay their staff enough. This is usually the problem with franchises that rely on young and cheap labor. With a drastically low minimum wage and the inability to tip your fast food attendee, these individuals work all day for insanely low amounts of money.

Have you ever heard the saying "You get what you pay for"? Inexperienced fast food staff make a lot of mistakes at the customer's expense. Worse yet are experienced staff that do not care, because they are not paid enough to care. To them, the job is mechanical and does not mean anything in their lives.

They show up at work, collect their paycheck, and do the absolute bare minimum to get by at work without being fired. This leads to widespread hygiene concerns, uncaring staff, and delays in operations and systematic efficiency. Franchises that do not pay well set the customer up for bad service.

For many of these under payers, the goal is not to build a cohesive, happy team that is well trained and ready to move up the ranks. Quite the opposite is true. In fact, staff turnover in these positions is very high, and inexperience is rife. I can outline a few examples of why this is a bad thing for the customer here.

If you ask for a cup of decaf coffee at a fast food restaurant and they do not have any, they will simply sell you normal coffee, claiming that it is decaf. It does not matter if you are allergic to caffeine or if you have a severe anxiety problem that is triggered by caffeinated coffee.

Fast food workers that are underpaid may also neglect to remove ingredients that you are allergic to, or they will lie to you about what is inside their food simply because it is too much trouble to find out. I have seen many servers walk into the "back" to ask the manager, wait for a moment or two, then walk out again and tell customers that "there aren't any."

When a franchise or restaurant[7] does not pay well, it means that their quality of staff declines. Service naturally declines after that, along with food preparation. A fry cook may not clean his grill often enough because it is a hassle. Oil may not be changed often enough, so food is contaminated with toxic substances from old oil.

You can always tell when people are underpaid. They look like they hate their jobs, and they hate you for interrupting their day and ordering something. This never bodes well for the customer. Servers and staff believe all the profit is going to the owner, and they feel taken advantage of. As a result, they actively do not care about their jobs.

Restaurants That Overwork Their Staff

Mistreatment of staff is the first thing to happen when a restaurant hits hard times and becomes in danger of losing money and closing. Employees take pay cuts and have to work longer hours to make up the time, or they are simply told to work for two shifts in a row. Because union status among restaurant staff is rare, they are often mistreated.

I am talking about staff that do not get sick days, so they are forced to work while they are heaving with flu—all over your delicious meal. Some 90% of restaurant staff in the U.S. are said to receive no sick days, no vacation time, and no health insurance. They are forced to be ill at work, and that is why when you eat out, sometimes you get sick later on.

Often restaurants engage in illegal tip pooling and wage theft, which forces employees to work longer hours for less. They wander around their shifts in a blind panic, making mistakes and delivering terrible service—not because they are bad at their jobs but because they are being exploited. Overworked staff do not have the energy to consider you.

---

7   *Subway Leads Fast Food Industry in Underpaying Workers, http://money.cnn. com/2014/05/01/news/economy/subway-labor-violations/*

Overworked staff[8] often become burnt out, which causes tension in the restaurant. Suddenly corners are being cut, food standards plummet, and the person that suffers is the customer—not the unethical owner. Customers do not get individual treatment, and they are lucky if they get the right food order.

An overworked bunch of people will be more likely to be rude to customers, will be short tempered, and will be prone to emotional breakdowns and worse. And not all customers are understanding. When employees are taken for granted and worked to the bone, it is not uncommon for tears to result. Because many of these individuals need their job, they suffer through it.

You can remedy this by making sure that you only eat at ethical restaurants that pay the staff a decent wage and never overwork them. You can always tell if staff are overworked because they appear stressed, worried, and unable to perform the simplest of tasks. This comes from overload, not being unable to actually do their jobs correctly.

Expect poor service like third-hand bread baskets uneaten by other customers, butter that has been topped up instead of replaced, and worse. This is how overworked staff save time and keep going despite the fact that they are exhausted. They have to learn to cut corners to survive in such a demanding job.

My advice would be to always keep a lookout for overworked staff. They are a clear indicator that all is not well with a restaurant. Servers should be calm, supportive, and friendly, not wound up, stressed, and sweaty. No one should have to run around to make the lowest federal minimum wage possible in the United States.

---

8   Kathleen Geier, *Why Are Working Conditions for Restaurant Employees So Bad?*, http://www.washingtonmonthly.com/political-animal-a/2013_03/why_are_working_conditions_for043617.php

Restaurants That Have No Customers

Most intelligent people are naturally suspicious of a restaurant at a peak hour that has no real customers to speak of. In fact, many people will refuse to walk into a restaurant if they do not see a general buzz of people in there. That is because of the huge variety of problems that result from poor customer turnover.

A few instances of this that I have experienced were enough to make me wary of dead restaurants forever. Two for one specials arise to get rid of over-ordered stock that is going old quickly. Staff are panicked because they are not earning enough in tips from paying customers. Strange new dishes may appear on the menu. While some people believe these dishes are "innovative" dishes to get more people in the restaurant, they are usually dishes made up of existing food to prevent financial loss. Anything stewed or covered in sauce is suspect in an empty restaurant. Sauces mask the taste of old meat, and stews can be flavored to hide the taste of the worst cuts imaginable.

You should also be wary of anything made in a large vat, even if that vat looks pretty and is covered in gold. A large coleslaw vat, for example, is the restaurant's way of saving money because it is not making any. That slaw will contain all the old vegetables imaginable; then it will be kept in the fridge covered in sauce for many, many days.

Along with the lack of stock rotation, there is also the possibility that sitting stock will give you extremely bad food poisoning. At least when a restaurant is busy, they are forced to use what stock they order. But a slow restaurant will contain food that was ordered for many people that just sits there.

When food sits at the wrong temperatures, it becomes contaminated with bacteria. That means your delicious fried chicken is actually salmonella chicken fried to mask the sliminess of it. Never ever order chicken or salad at a slow restaurant! The lack of customers should be a clue that something is very wrong with their food.

The harsh thing is that most of the time the restaurant is slow because it is not being run correctly. That means you not only have the old food to contend with but the lack of hygiene, operational standards, and quality of service that you should expect as well.

And finally, the most suspect of all is the buffet at a low turnover restaurant. This is when everything remaining in the kitchen has been cooked or disguised, and you can now eat it to help the restaurant keep its doors open. The only little hitch might be that everything is going bad, has gone bad, or will make you incredibly sick. Pick carefully!

Restaurants That Are Short Staffed

How does the joke go—don't eat at a restaurant on the moon; it has no atmosphere! Jokes aside, you should never eat at a restaurant that is short staffed. This is because there may be menu changes in place to help the staff cope with the overburden of having too many people to serve and too many dishes to cook.

Perhaps the worst of all is a short-staffed restaurant that is also extremely busy. The cooks can be replaced with front of house staff, with inexperienced servers now in the kitchen putting the recipes together. The cooks may also have to alter the menu, replacing complex dishes with heat and eat dishes.

Short-staffed restaurants are terrible, and I have worked in several of them. Customers are ferried to their tables without so much as a smile, there is way too much nervous energy around, and mistakes cause frustration and poor service. When a place is short staffed, even a small mistake can seem like a mountain.

With frustrated staff, customers can easily become frustrated as well. If you see this is happening, cut them some slack, or go somewhere else. It is impossible to enjoy a dining out "experience" when all you are experiencing is the poor planning of the restaurant manager. Everything from the food you order to the service that you get could be impacted.

Worse yet is that because one poor server will be running around to ten different tables, the chances of any orders coming out correctly are slim. They will forget items and replacements and get your order wrong. Then they will compensate and end up having to pay out of pocket for their mistakes.

When you are at a short-staffed[9] restaurant with overly busy staff, you should become highly suspicious of all specials that are running. These will be the lowest quality food items that the servers have been told to push to save time for the kitchen. The result is that you will get your "cheap" steak and chips that do not taste nice but only took five minutes to make.

Never forget that the restaurant's main goal is to keep functioning, which means that the things that they recommend to you are more in their best interest than yours. With a lack of staff comes a lack of quality, hygiene, and rushed service.

Proximity Alerts: Do Not Eat Food Here!

There are a lot of good times to eat at a restaurant and a lot of bad times to eat at a restaurant. If you are going to a new place for the first time, avoid these times to optimize your eating out experience. You will be much better off for it!

- Do not eat at a restaurant when they are super busy. Your service will be second rate, and your food might be rushed just for the sake of getting it out. A rushed cook skips doing things properly to keep dishes flying out of the kitchen. The result is an overly busy service and food that is not quite as good as it could be.

---

9   Sam Ashe-Edmunds, *What Do You Do When You Have a Short Staff in the Kitchen*, http://yourbusiness.azcentral.com/short-staff-kitchen-10544.html

- Do not eat at a popular tourist restaurant in tourist season. Many tourist town residents do not bother to eat there when it is peak season. This is because the staff is usually overworked, prices are higher, and food quality suffers for the sake of turning tables. Tourist hotspots are more about quantity than quality in peak season.
- Avoid restaurants[10] with visibly poor hygiene. If the front of house is bad, the back of house is going to be terrible. They are happy to let you see the mess in the front, which means that whatever is hidden is far, far worse. If the environment smells old or moldy and is dust or pest ridden, get out.
- Opening time at a restaurant is not the ideal time to eat there. Staff are still busy preparing the food for the day, and they may need to move items that have been sitting for a while. That means they will get served to the first few customers they have. If you want fresher food, come midday.
- Closing time at a restaurant is not the ideal time to eat there either. Many items may be near expiration or need to be finished before the next morning, which means that you will get them. At the same time, the staff are tired and totally all right with cutting corners. They just want to go home after a long shift.
- Do not eat out on holidays, because it will be overly crowded, and standards will drop. Whatever you do, do not order the special. It is there to speed things along and will be a heat and eat dish to prep for the rush. Plus, you will have to wait a very long time for your food, even if it is a simple dish.
- Do not sit in high traffic areas in a restaurant, or your food will contain more bacteria that anywhere else on the front of the house floor. Never sit near the bathrooms, and try to find a spot by good ventilation so that you do not sit near any damp or unclean areas hidden away in a corner somewhere.

---

10 Anthony Bourdain, *Things to Avoid When Eating in Restaurants*, http://www. theguardian.com/books/2000/aug/12/features.weekend1

What Not to Eat at a Restaurant

CHAPTER 3
THE RESTAURANT YOU HAVE CHOSEN

"When you go to a restaurant, the less you know about what happens in the kitchen, the more you enjoy your meal."

JEFFREY WRIGHT

Restaurants can be like minefields, or they can be a pure delight to enjoy. Being able to tell the difference in food quality at a restaurant is a skill that everyone should develop. After all, the responsibility rests on the customers to decide what they will order and devour.

In this chapter, I am going to use my extensive experience working in all areas of a restaurant—from cooking, cleaning, serving, and running, to managing staff and customers—so that you can get a firm grip on how to assess a restaurant and its menu items.

Assessing the Environment

It is time to unleash your inner restaurant[11] critic. Restaurant hopping is a common hobby for friends, family, and pleasure-seeking couples looking for a good time. One of the most reinvigorating things in life is experiencing new things, and this is a fun way to test something new while not having to cook or clean anything afterwards.

Here is how I assess a new restaurant when I come barreling through the doors looking for a good time, a great meal, and some excellent service. A restaurant is made up of three things: reputation, first impressions, and lasting memories. A superb restaurant nails all three of these consistently and may even become a favorite hangout of yours.

- **Reputation**: Online and offline, restaurants these days cannot hide from the truth. People eat there, and then they share their experiences. It is up to you to make sure that your chosen location has a solid reputation. Check before you choose, or check before you walk into a new place that has intrigued you.

Use TripAdvisor, Eater.com, Zagat.com, and Yelp.com as research sources.

- **First Impressions**: These count more than you may think! Stale, musty curtains are a surprisingly accurate indicator of stale, musty food. Look at the décor, breathe in the smell of the place, and notice how staff bustle around cleaning—do they even use soap or just a dirty, germ-ridden cloth? Your environment matters.

Watch out for bored-looking staff. Restaurants should always be busy because there is a never-ending list of things to do. Bored staff

---

11 *Elizabeth C., How to Review a Restaurant Like a Pro!, http://thedish.restaurant. com/how-to-review-a-restaurant-like-a-pro/*

means poor management, which leads to the dark side of quality control.

- **Lasting Memories**: Try everything once, I always say. Give that place a fair chance to impress critical, cynical you. You deserve the best, but can they give it to you? Engage in the ambiance, and drink your fill of the experience—from the people to the food, the service, the music, and the general vibe. Did you have fun?

A brilliant restaurant experience will keep you coming back. It is always a combination of factors that unify to create a wonderful dining-out event. And it should be an "event" because you are not just paying for some cooked food to keep you alive!

Tables and Table Settings

Think of your restaurant table as your own private piece of restaurant real estate. You are renting it during your eating experience. It is the central location where you will enjoy the finest comfort, food, and service that the place has to offer. Plus, it will impact your overall perspective and help you decide whether or not to return to that eatery.

First, and arguably the most important, is the location of your table. Like in real estate, it is wise to choose less trafficked areas for positioning. Do not sit near a bathroom or close to the main serving counter. Now it is time to assess your chosen home for the next two hours.

Your table may or may not have been wiped down. The towel could have been filthy; you just do not know. Assume that a lack of cleaning product smell means it is not clean. The busser is a slave to the restaurant system, which demands fast work, and a sanitizing system. These systems almost always fail to change cloths regularly.

The dirtiest places on the table are the edges, the condiment area, and the chairs you are sitting on. A tablecloth is a great sign, as long as it is clean. No tablecloths means rampant germs and an easy way to hide bad cleaning practices. In an average restaurant, there are never enough tablecloths—which means they may simply be shaken out.

Many restaurants fail to change their tablecloths[12] as much as they should. A stain is gross, but discoloration and several stains is a key warning sign that dodgy food is ahead. Lots of these are simply scraped for crumbs or flipped. Notice the edges. You can always tell how often a tablecloth is washed by the aging edges.

The place settings can also tell you a thing or two about the restaurant you have chosen. Silverware is usually washed in a flat rack, ideally without ramekins, scoops, or larger utensils thrown into it. It needs to be individually placed, not lumped together. Too many places are happy to clean off excess food after the "wash" with the drying cloths.

Silverware rolling is a tedious task, and there are always quotas to fill. That means lots of handling as it becomes a competitive sport for the staff. Done at the end of the day, this is something that needs to be banged out because staff are anxious to get home. They scrape off whatever food remains and wrap it up in a neat, dirty package.

Silverware should also be dried with a clean rag, which is rarely the case. I have seen a guest's dirty napkin taken from a laundry bag and used more than once. Cutlery wrapped in tissue paper is cleaner, as the cloth napkins may not be washed as often as you would hope. These are the trappings of the table where you are seated!

---

12 *Cleanliness: The Restaurant Table, http://directorslounge.hubpages.com/hub/ Cleanliness-The-Restaurant-Table*

The Menu & Condiments

Next up are the menu and condiment areas. Both are touched by all the customers that enter that restaurant and the staff too. The most disturbing thing about these two specific items is that they are a magnet for babies and toddlers.

I have seen hundreds of kids suck on menus, salt and pepper shakers, packet sugar, ketchup bottles, or whatever else happens to be in front of them on that table. They suck it, and then their moms put it back. There you are—all the germs you could want with an extra helping of toddler spittle. Gross!

Customers also sometimes have trouble seeing the difference between a menu and a placemat. They love to stack their drippy cups and leaky plates on them, and believe me, they are not wiped clean as often as they should be. Once a day is great, but it is rare.

More hands touch them than the peanut dish; they are slabs of germ colonies waiting to invade your system. It might be wise to carry some anti-bacterial wipes around with you if your immune system is low and you need to stay contamination-free.

Condiments are like little pacifiers for children. I am always amazed by the mothers that allow their babies to suck on strange things they found on the table. Not only is it super disgusting but it is hazardous to the child. Not so long ago there we use to "marry" glass bottles of ketchup. You would gather up all the used bottles of ketchup and combine them by tapping them together. This resulted in chipped bottles and really old ketchup. Sometimes you could hear a bottle explode from across the room. Thankfully, that practice is all but dead.

These days you get the packets or disposable plastic bottles, which is a lot more hygienic. If there is still a glass bottle on the table, beware. There is a good chance it is the germiest thing in the restaurant. The same goes for the packets; people often pick them up, play with them, then put them back.

Tearing one open with your teeth invites all those hand germs inside your mouth! Viruses and bacteria can last for up to 18 hours[13] on hard surfaces, and that is a fact.

The salt and pepper shakers on your table can be tough to clean, and more often than not, they are not cleaned enough. You can tell by looking at them. If the salt sticks, beware! Many patrons have unscrewed the lid and dipped their fingers in there to loosen it up. In general, be wary of table sauces, what they contain, and their level of cleanliness.

You can tell a lot about a restaurant by the state of their menu and condiments. If your menu is clean and dry—along with your table sauces—great. But if they are not, then you have to question what else is being overlooked, ignored, and glanced over.

Charger Plates & Glasses

Two of the most suspect items for assessment on your restaurant outing have to be the charger plates and glasses that you will use. A charger plate is a simple decorative plate that usually goes beneath your main plates that you will eat off of.

Because charger plates are decorative, they tend to go for many days—even weeks—without being washed at all. I have seen lots of restaurants give them a quick wipe down with the restaurant rag, all ready for the next patron.

The problem with this is that these plates can harbor more germs than nearly anything else at your table, depending on the restaurant you are visiting. The only way to be sure that they are clean is to sterilize them yourself.

To check these charger plates, lift them into the air to see if there are fingerprint marks anywhere by glancing light off them.

---

13 Lindsay Goldwert, 7 Germiest Places; Germs Lurk on Menus, Lemon Wedges, Condiment and Soap Dispensers, http://www.nydailynews.com/life-style/health/7-germiest-places-germs-lurk-menus-lemon-wedges-condiment-soap-dispensers-article-1.469626

Fingerprints, smears, and hard, dried food are a sure sign that they need to be cleaned. Otherwise, they should be okay because they do not touch your food. You never eat from them, which is a bonus.

To be safe, I would also be suspicious of your bread and butter plates and other unused utensils on your table. Often these rotate between many guests, being used over and over if they "appear" to be unused. Of course, anyone can sneeze into a napkin, touch things with dirty hands, or worse without leaving any visible evidence of it.

If you have a pitcher of water on your table, leave it where it stands. Instead, order a bottle of water that is sealed. Chances are the open-air water is old or a mixture of new and old, which is even worse. Service staff love to take shortcuts when filling these, so they will speed through it, cutting lemon wedges[14] and tossing them in.

The result, however, is water that is not fresh, clean, or good tasting. Glasses that are unused should be dishwasher clear, without fingerprints. If residue remains, it has not been washed but lightly rinsed. And beware of the restaurant where they clean glasses by huffing into them to create steam for polishing!

Typically, you should sit down and not feel like your table was recently the location of a kid's party. If it is not fresh and clean, it does not bode well for your dining choice. As a rule, the hygiene in the front of the house is infinitely better than the back.

The Setup in the Back

Let's talk about the backend of the restaurant, the one you cannot see. I believe the more you can see, the better. That is why it has been proven that restaurants with visible food preparation areas from the dining room are cleaner and healthier.

---

14 *Laura Schocker, This Will Make You Never, Ever Want to Put a Lemon Wedge in Your Water Again, http://www.huffingtonpost.com/2014/01/27/lemon-germs-wedges-restaurants_n_4659168.html*

The setup in the back is very important for the overall restaurant experience. Think about it! Service staff need to be able to move around in there. Food needs to be stored, prepared, and cooked in there. People have to be able to work hard and practice hygiene there.

If you want an impression of the restaurant, take a quick peek into their back of house. Look for a sink and signs promoting hand washing. Look for clean aprons, disposable gloves, and clean surfaces. Check if the floor is clean or has a lot of places where pests could hide.

What you want is a flowing kitchen that is clean and easy to work in for the staff. This goes a long way in helping great food come out of that kitchen. It is also wise to use your nose when you walk past. If you smell old oil, burnt food, or an overwhelming chemical smell, it should be a bit of a red flag.

One thing that is non-negotiable is the sink. There has to be one in the kitchen; otherwise, all of the food is contaminated. Chefs sweat, kitchen staff get ill and touch loads of things during the day, and when service is busy, if the sink is not close by, it does not get used. Not to mention all the horrible sweat that people whip up during their shift.

As a distinguished customer, you deserve a healthy restaurant ecosystem in the kitchen. This is where your food is being cooked. If it is full of old food, dirt, and lazy staff, your chances of getting delicious food are zero. Rotation is the key to an energized, happy kitchen. Poor management, bad practices, and unmotivated staff can trash that ideal.

Urgency[15] and precision make a kitchen great. If the staff have time to lean, then they have time to clean. If the place is filthy and they are leaning, it puts your experience at risk.

---

15 Dan Gentile, *Things You Have to Explain to People Who've Never Worked in Kitchens*, http://www.thrillist.com/eat/nation/understanding-cooks-best-kitchen-advice

The Setup in the Front

The front of house, as people in the restaurant business call it, is the space where the customers enjoy their dining experience. Your table and everything around it is your special front of house space, and it should be up to standards.

When entering a restaurant for the first time, there are some quick checks that you can use to assess if the restaurant is good enough to settle down to. The first is the exterior of the building and the signage. It should be clean, well maintained, and inviting. The same can be said of the inside. There should be no odors, and fresh air should permeate the space.

Good ventilation is always a decent sign because it means more alert staff that will not feel so claustrophobic. Notice how you are treated when you enter. Expect a warm greeting, eye contact, and an attempt to make you feel welcome. The staff should be proactive, not hanging around waiting for something to do or chatting to each other.

Too much chatting from the staff leads to poor service for the customers as they become distracted and do not keep an eye on their tables. The furniture should be sturdy and the table tops clean and fresh. Take a look around the place, especially at the walls and standing décor. You want them to be dust and fingerprint free.

Clean floors means that someone has taken the time to ensure that despite the constant traffic, hygiene is important. You can also tell by the attitudes of the staff what the restaurant is like. If they seem unhappy, bored, or unwilling to help, you should assume that your experience will be similar to theirs.

The front of a restaurant should exemplify the attitude and vibe of the place. A bright, cheery, busy bistro is always going to have better food and service than a dank, slow, musty one. Do not be afraid to ask your server questions about the restaurant and the story behind the place too. You can learn a lot by listening in on what they think about working there.

Finally, it helps to keep a formal log on your experience. That means leaving reviews! Not only will you help future diners find better restaurant experiences but you will be able to look back and see if you genuinely enjoyed an experience or not. This can be invaluable for future visits, especially if, like me, you love to go restaurant hunting.

CHAPTER 4

ROACHES AND RATS: THE TRUTH

> *"We hope that, when the insects take over the world, they will remember with gratitude how we took them along on all our picnics."*
>
> BILL VAUGHAN

The very first day I begin work at a new restaurant, I will peer under the coffee machine for clues about their hygiene practices. I am not really looking for roaches during the day, although I sometimes find them if the place is far dirtier than it should be.

Machines in confined spaces are a great test to see what kind of pests the restaurant has attracted. It is not uncommon to find crusty coffee grounds and liquid spills there—the perfect lure for roaches and rats. You can tell a lot about a restaurant by the pests they feed, and by "feed," I mean ignoring proper hygiene and not getting the pest van in.

Foods That Pests Love

Pests are everywhere. They come in the form of small, creepy, crawly insects; large, fluttery, fast scuttlers; or sneaky stealth mammals. Whatever their form, everyone hates them. All restaurants have their pest problems, no matter how clean they are.

Some restaurants have no control over this, because there are neighboring eateries with pest problems that are never solved. The pests leak over into their properties, and it becomes an ongoing battle. The thing that attracts the pests to their locations, however, is the food they leave lying around.

Pests[16] just love sticky, sugary, sweet foods, and they cannot wait to infest the areas of the restaurant that are rich in these goodies. Food storage is a big concern because improper handling of these foods creates a bug buffet.

That old apple cider in the trash with the mounds of rinds and bits of old meat will attract roaches and rats to the place super quickly. Above all, pests love food that is left unattended, and they are not picky about its age or odor.

Most pests will eat just about anything left in the corner, under hard to reach cleaning zones, neglected ovens, and fridges. Their favorite is the dreaded soda machine, which is why I make a point of drinking bottled drinks in a restaurant. Pest infestations will be easier to spot at night, and teams should be called in to deal with severe problems.

Restaurant Hiding Places

Where in the restaurant do these wonderful little scurrying and crawly friends like to hide? Everywhere is the short answer. The longer answer is that they are masters of stealth, having developed an aversion for human handling over the past few centuries.

---

16 *A Bug's Love Affair With Food, http://www.mybugproblem.com/blog/a-bugs-love-affair-with-food-benton-pest-control*

Just because a restaurant appears to be pest free does not mean that it is. On the other hand, if flies and roaches are running free, this is not a good sign. It means that the infestation is out of control and little is being done about it. You can bet a lot of the food is contaminated at that point. Roaches, especially, like to stay hidden.

Pests love to take up residence where their food lives. If there are places to hide, lots of food left around, and poor hygiene practices, you can bet there are creatures living there. Here are some of the hot spots where pests like to take up residence.

- *Dry food storage areas are like snack bars for pests.* They love the boxes, the packets, and the half-opened food packages. If the restaurant has pests, they will likely also be in their main food storage areas.

- *The walk-in fridge!* You would think that the cold would scare them away, but alas, that is not the case. Roaches and rats do not care about a little chill. They will casually infest the walk-in, stealing food when they can sneak past during normal daily traffic. They usually take up residence in the kitchen for easy access.

- *Storage and receiving areas.* Roaches[17] and other pests love to hitch rides in boxes, on crates, and in delivery packages. Just one infested delivery and the kitchen can become a roach nightmare within a few short weeks. Keeping the receiving areas of the restaurant clean and tidy is critical to maintaining a pest-free zone.

- *Underneath hard-to-reach areas.* This includes places like under ovens, under ice machines, under soft-serve ice cream machines, and behind built-in appliances. If you fail to move things around and clean inside and around them, they will become pest homes. The pest super highway runs behind things and underneath them!

---

17 Dr. Anil Menon, *Pest Management in Restaurants, http://pestcontrol.basf.us/news-&-events/feature-stories/archive/pest-management-in-restaurants.pdf*

- *Restaurant waste should be removed from the premises quickly so that pests cannot convert that area into a fast food zone for themselves.* The longer the waste sits, the greater the chance that it will attract pests. Restaurant waste should be taken outside, far from the food preparation area, and sealed tightly in bags.

Why Pest Control Is a Good Thing

One thing I learned about restaurants that customers do not realize is that the presence of the "pest control" van is a good sign. It is common for customers to see the van and be discouraged from going to that restaurant again.

This is the opposite of what should happen! Seeing the van outside is one of the best things you can see. First of all, it does not necessarily mean that the restaurant is brimming with roaches and rats and that you are going to be served worm soup with roach legs in it.

In fact, many, many restaurant owners will want to nip any roach or rodent infestation in the bud by getting the professionals in to maintain high standards of hygiene and safety. So when you see the pest control van, you know that the manager of that place cares about their customers and is taking care of the pests that they have found.

The alternative is horrifying—managers that use pesticides themselves, contaminating the air quality in the kitchen and food areas and generally making the problem worse and the environment less than sanitary. I believe that seeing a van is a great sign of responsibility. If you see a roach and never see a van, that is when suspicion should be aroused.

Pest control[18] happens to all restaurants. We live in the world,

---

18 *Pests Share Hot Spots & Solutions, http://facilitymanagement.com/articles/ maintenance-2013-06-4.html*

after all, where urban pests are a problem for everyone. Every restaurant that has ever existed has had to deal with these pests at one time or another, whether they have five-star levels of hygiene or not.

Change your mindset on seeing the pest control van. It is not a negative thing! It actually means that the restaurant will no longer have a pest control problem in the near future, and best of all, they did it correctly and safely by bringing in professionals. That means all nooks and crannies will be factored in.

I get very suspicious of places when I go there often, see the occasional pest, and never see them dealing with it. A roach trap in the bathroom, for example, is a wonderful example of a manager trying to cut corners and deal with a serious problem incorrectly. This is when you should be grossed out and never come back.

As for the van itself, wave to them when you see them. They do a good job of keeping us all safe from poisons, pests, and contamination—and it can be thankless work.

The Location & Operations

I love to probe into the hygiene of a restaurant I am working at to see how they deal with pests and cleanliness. Often a lazy manager will yell at staff when they bring these things to their attention. Bad managers are usually the direct cause of operational failure and the ability for pests to infest and take hold at a location.

After a few weeks of working at a place, I will inspect the ice tea pourer—a job any solid dishwashing department should do regularly. Often it will be so filled with gunk that you will wonder how you even have been getting it to pour tea. From there, I go to the coffee machine, attempting to tilt it back from the front. If I am lucky, it will come right up or stick just slightly. Other times it can require some strength as you hear it peeling from the dark, old spillage and grounds. Add the heat of the machine, and it makes a darn good place for a family of roaches to sleep.

Next up for my gruesome inspection is the soda machine, which, depending on the grossness of what I have found so far and the questioning looks from various staff members, might be left for another day. It can be disgusting work thanks to the sweetness of the machine and the pests it attracts. So when I do move over to the soda[19] machine covers, I prepare for flight. All sorts of things come scuttling out of that machine.

The moment a cover is popped off, you know what the place is like at night when everyone has gone home. Either nothing will come out (a great sign) or a hundred tiny cockroaches will fall down in roach raindrops fleeing in every direction, even up your arms.

They will dash to the ice bin, crawling over you in the process and escaping to anywhere there is not light. It can be a nightmare. Something I really respect is when a road of restaurant businesses band together to deal with a neighborhood pest problem. Trying to kill roaches when surrounding businesses are full of them is useless.

Managers that band together to take care of the issue get it done. The pest control vans show up in force and clean up the entire street. That works like a charm, but it takes organization skills from the manager and a certain degree of humility. No restaurant wants to admit that they have pests, but worse than that is fighting a losing battle.

Quarterly visits from a pest control provider are paramount to customer safety. To see if a restaurant operates efficiently, look around. Are there pests outside? In neighboring zones? Does the interior of the restaurant seem clean and chemical free? There should not be traps, chemicals, and pollutants lying around.

There is a common saying in the restaurant niche that if a neighbor has pests, so do you. It can help to research the

---

19 *Foods Pests Love, http://www.holderspestsolutions.com/blog/post/foods-pests-love*

surrounding restaurants to get a read on the state of the restaurant you want to experience that evening. Complaints and poor reviews from surrounding places is never a good sign!

The Drinks of Roach Wrath

Now for a little more gross cockroach investigation before I can let you move on to less disgusting areas in a restaurant. Bars are a particularly bad location for cockroaches because of all the dark places, the often rampantly poor hygiene practices, and the mounds of sugar, sweet drinks, and mixers that attract them.

To a cockroach, a bar is like an oasis of their favorite things to eat and drink. Plus, they get to shack up in a nice, dark place with lots of hiding places. They never have to face people ever! This is why bars can be so disgusting. Ever been in a random bar and seen a roach scuttle past you? One means there are lots and lots more.

There is no such thing as a cockroach without a large family in tow. They breed quickly and consistently, and they are master scavengers. Like icebergs, what you see is only the very tip of the problem. For every one you spot, there may be fifty you are not seeing. Gross!

The reason why you tend to see roaches in bars more often than in restaurants is because of the constant sugary alcohol spills. Everything is sticky and wet, and roaches like warmth and moisture. Plus, they are not picky eaters. If all there is to eat is leftovers, crumbs, and bar snacks, they will live off these, just like they can live off sewerage, trash, and bark.

A bar with a roach[20] problem may also have a straw problem because roaches like to lay their eggs in them. Always check your drinks straw before you sip through it to see if there are small, black eggs inside it. Assume that all bars have roaches, no matter how high end they are. Just because you are not seeing them does not mean that they are not there.

---

20 *Cockroach Food, http://www.orkin.com/cockroaches/cockroach-food/*

Roaches like to hide underneath the drinks fridges, in the ice machine, under counters, along skirting boards, in cabinets, and in appliances. If the bar has a slop bucket, or a place where they can empty out drinks, expect roaches to be nesting there. Due to these little critters always being on location, I far prefer to drink from sealed bottles.

You will not believe how they get into draft beer areas, crawl over open bottles and jugs of things, and generally find ways to get into open-air products like ice, lemon wedges, and other drink garnishes. Beware of the cocktail with many garnishes. You can bet your boots that at some point either a roach, fly, gnat, or dirty hands touched that bar fruit.

Where the Rats Like to Play

Let's get it out there—rats are disgusting. Humans developed an outright fear for them when they nearly killed all of us back in the old days. Heard of the plague? You can thank a major rat problem for that dark period in our history. They carry all sorts of horrifying diseases and can infest restaurants just as easily as roaches can.

Whenever I start at a new restaurant, I like to do a rat check. The first place I begin is the dry foods storage area, especially if it is located in a separate room. Oh, how rats love to enjoy the dry foods in a room away from the hustle and bustle of service! By giving them their privacy, they feel free to move right in.

Along with roaches, rats have a powerful sweet tooth. They are not afraid to take what they can and eat everything in sight. The first signs of a rat problem are the little poops they leave behind, usually accompanied by gnaw marks on boxes and packets. Unlike roaches, rats are perfectly capable of opening up large, sealed boxes, thank you very much.

All bets are off when you take a consignment of dry goods and stash it in the back for a while, thinking it is safe. It usually is not. These goods need to be checked regularly, rotated, and secured against rats and roaches. Rats love to get inside your walls and run along skirting boards and in attic ceilings.

Rice and sugar are their favorite foods, and they will stop at nothing to get to them. There is a very strong odor associated with a rat infestation, and once you know it, you will be able to recognize it for life. If you see random rat traps in a restaurant, beware. It means that the owner is not willing to shell out for adequate pest control.

A 2013 Harvard study[21] proved that 77 out of 154 eateries on the Upper East Side in New York were infested with rats. So it is a lot more common than you think. Even though rats can be large, they have the ability to squeeze into tiny spaces, making entry possible nearly anywhere in your average restaurant.

Plus, like cockroaches, they breed quickly and can unleash a world of hygiene hell in a reasonably clean restaurant that had no problems before. The trick is to always focus on hygiene and to look out for the common signs of these pests at the eatery you choose. One sighting is a roach or rat too many. Remember that!

---

21 *Frank Rosario, Selim Algar, Half of Upper East Side Restaurants Are Rat Infested: Study, http://nypost.com/2014/02/18/half-of-upper-east-side-restaurants-are-rat-infested-study/*

CHAPTER 5
THE STAFF ALARM

> "Employees are a company's greatest asset—they're your competitive advantage. You want to attract and retain the best; provide them with encouragement, stimulus, and make them feel that they are an integral part of the company's mission."
>
> — ANNE M. MULCAHY

I have worked with some amazing teams over the years and some not so amazing ones. It has always amused me how some people can care so much about what they do and others could not give a fig. In every restaurant, there are interesting staff practices, from hiring and firing, to habits, breaks, and upselling.

The things that go on in these restaurants would curl your toes! I am not telling you these industry secrets to scare you but more to alert you to what can and does happen when you wander into a new restaurant. Be aware that not everything is as it seems.

How Staff Is Commonly Hired

There are thousands of wait staff, managers, and other restaurant personnel in the industry, and they all have different agendas. Some range from temporary, part-time workers that are seasonal and only want to get through their shift, while others are professionals that want to retire at the top of their game in the restaurant business.

Not all restaurants have excellent hiring practices, even though the average customer expects it. So many restaurants[22] are family owned and operated that the staff is hired using a special blend of "who they know" and "what is easy." This combines into a staff that is often young, inexperienced, and, quite frankly, not very good at their jobs.

In many restaurants around the United States, staff are hired for personal reasons. Tom was made the manager of the restaurant because he is the owner's best friend. No, he has no prior restaurant management experience. Suzy and Lucy are the waitresses in the restaurant because they were the first two that replied to the ad.

Or they were friends of the owner's daughter. Or they are his cousins. There is a lot of nepotism in the restaurant field, which is great until you see the issues it causes. When you hire someone because of who they are instead of how they work, problems arise. Bad service, poor food, an uncaring attitude, laziness, and shortcuts are rife.

Then there is the inadequate training that trickles down the line. A bad, inexperienced manager has no idea how to train inexperienced wait staff. An unqualified chef might make good food but not during peak service—because they have no idea how to run a kitchen. Staff is commonly hired via this "who they know" process.

---

22 Frances Burks, *The Effects of Bad Hiring in a Restaurant, http://smallbusiness. chron.com/effects-bad-hiring-restaurant-36458.html*

The White Lies Staff Tell

Next up on the staff alarm menu are the white lies. A white lie is a lie that does not necessarily hurt anyone, but it is still a complete falsehood. These can be quite common in poorly managed and poorly run restaurants. I know because I have seen it happen firsthand many times and in a lot of different scenarios.

It is a given that when a customer walks into a nice restaurant, they expect to ask the wait staff questions and get honest answers in return. But this is not always reality. In fact, there can be hundreds of little white lies that make up a day. This blows the perception out of the water that wait staff are supportive, helpful, and honest individuals.

I have seen many people ask for coffee, and be served decaf, especially at the end of the night when they are cleaning up. Twenty minutes before closing time many places do not want to make two pots of coffee, one decaf and one regular, to sell two cups. Some restaurants I have worked at do not even carry coffee, only decaf. No one can tell. In part, it is cheaper and easier, but also you are then not responsible for staff switching unsuspecting customers to caffeine-laden coffee if that person has trouble with anxiety and caffeine.

Then there are the "specials." When certain food gets old and the manager decides to run a special, the staff is told to push that dish.

Then when you invite them to recommend "something good," or "interesting," or "different," the waiters will automatically invite you to enjoy the special. They will tell you nearly anything to get you to order it because it is what their boss wants. They do not want you to know that you are ordering older food with a time clock that is running out.

And they definitely do not want you to know that the dish may not be the "delicious, interesting, different" thing that you asked for. Upselling[23] is a wonderful opportunity for wait staff to dish out white lies. They will not pay attention to your experience at all, instead working off the demands of their boss and the needs of the restaurant.

Also be aware that some wait staff are given quotas. They are told to sell additional items, and many do this in a deceitful way. By the time your bill comes, you realize those seemingly complimentary fries and veggies were all add-ons with a hefty price tag. At that point, there is little to be done but pay. Never be afraid to ask if recommended extras will be charged.

Allergies and Distasteful Foods

There is some confusion among customers when it comes to telling their wait staff what foods they can and cannot eat. I believe the disconnect happens because customers believe that to emphasize their distaste for some foods, they have to lie and say that they are highly allergic to them, which can be destructive.

"Yes, is there any wheat or gluten in that? I cannot eat that. No, highly allergic. I will simply get so ill if I eat it," the customer will say. The problem is that when customers do this, it desensitizes wait staff to what really happens when people are allergic to something.

The downside of this can be catastrophic. Wait staff may lie about certain foods not being in the ingredient list, which seems fine because most of the time, "distaste" does not make people ill. However, when a person with a real allergy expressly asks for that food to be left off their plate or asks to make sure that it is not in the ingredient list, things can happen.

Thinking that it is just another "distaste" customer, the wait staff will once again lie about a critical ingredient, and this will result in a hospital visit for the customer. Never tell your waiter that you

---

23 Robert Sietsema, *Why I Hate Upselling in Restaurants, and the Emergence of Narrative Upselling*, http://www.villagevoice.com/restaurants/why-i-hate-upselling-in-restaurants-and-the-emergence-of-narrative-upselling-6555268

are deathly allergic to lettuce if you are not; it disrespects people that are genuinely allergic to things. Then, when they make a valid request or ask a valid question, they pay for it.

You might believe that the onus is on the wait staff member to always do what they are asked, but this is not the case. During a busy service, they may ask an overwhelmed manager, a new shift supervisor, or a busy cook and get a generic answer. This happens because so many people insist that they have allergies.

It creates the impression that everyone is lying and that corners can be cut. And they often are—resulting in terrible experiences for genuine allergy sufferers. Big allergies[24] like nuts and gluten might be taken more seriously, but for the lesser known foods—onions, vegetables, and other "strange" allergies—it is better to be honest.

It is perfectly fine to say, "I do not like onions in my food, thanks," and expect the waiter to remove them from the dish. If you want to order the soup but there may be onions in it, it is better to divert to something more obvious—or you risk becoming an enabler.

Staff Uniform Troubles

Wait staff are made to wear uniforms to show the customer that they are part of the restaurant team. It helps them display unity and teamwork and shows the customer that they are smart, ready for action, and organized.

At least that is what uniforms do in a well-managed restaurant. If you happen to find yourself eating at a restaurant with management troubles, then that may not be the case. It is not uncommon to see wait staff with dirty uniforms because they failed to wash them from the day before.

---

24   Colette Bouchez, *Food Allergies: Tips for Eating Out*, *http://www.webmd.com/ allergies/features/food-allergies-tips-for-eating-out*

One of the most common complaints on sites like TripAdvisor and Yelp are about smelly waiters. These individuals smell funky after one service, but then they do not wash their uniform for three or four shifts in a row. The result is a trail of smell coming off the waiter that makes the customers want to be ill.

Different people sweat at different paces and smell at different levels too. But the bottom line is that uniforms should be washed daily, whether they contain smell and stains or not. This is not an easy rule to enforce at a busy restaurant, where sweat and smell can happen over the course of three hours in some cases.

No one in the world wants to be served food from a person that reeks like a skunk. It puts them off their food and makes the restaurant look really bad. This is sad when the food there is rather good and the hygiene practices are high. Just one stinky waiter and a bad review can tank a new restaurant that opens in the USA. People do not like bad smells.

Then there are the aprons! Unwashed aprons[25] are a bane for wait staff, but it is really easy to forget to wash them. A clean uniform with a dirty apron is redundant. Worse yet are the implements that come out of the dirty, seven-day-unwashed apron: spare cutlery, your bill, pens, notepads, straws, sweets, wet-naps, phones, and more.

A waiter's apron can be like Mary Poppins' bag or a wizard's magic hat. But everything inside it is contaminated and totally dirty. That means their hands are dirty, along with everything they touch—including your plates, glasses, and food. It is better to watch out for these serial unwashed aprons and to insist on hygiene for your own safety.

---

25   Tracy Jong, *Obstacles for Restaurant Uniforms, http://tracyjonglawfirm.com/ rwlblog/?p=240*

The Truth About Gloves

Here is a startling truth that you may not know about. There is a long-standing myth that cooks and kitchen staff that wear gloves are somehow "cleaner" than those that do not. The myth began because direct hand-to-food touching was considered gross.

Of course, in the real world, gloves mean nothing. If you put dirty hands into gloves then wear them, they will become twice as dirty as your hands. Even worse, the filth inside the gloves mixes with sweat and congeals, becoming gritty and grimy. These bits can end up in your food! Gloves have been proven to be less clean than hands.

You have to wash your hands regularly and be aware of the things that you touch during food preparation. The problem comes in when cooks think that gloves have some kind of magical power to protect them against dirt and germs. All the gloves do is keep their hands from touching it, but they still touch it. Then they touch your food.

I have seen kitchen staff take out the trash wearing gloves then continue to chop vegetables for inclusion in a soup. And I have seen worse things than this! Gloves seem to make people believe they are cleaner without that being the case. In fact, it may trick kitchen staff into thinking that they can touch more dirt because they are somehow protected.

The reality is that gloves are filthy, especially when they are used for long periods of time. I have seen some people wash their disposable gloves like they are washing their hands instead of taking two seconds and getting a new pair. In every way possible, gloves are unhygienic. Sure, in a doctor's surgery in a sterile environment, they have their uses. Then they are disposed of properly.

But for general food preparation and cooking, this is not the case. Those same gloved hands touch the utensils, the pot and pan handles, the surfaces, the cabinets, the floors, and more. It was recently proven[26] that even the best gloves are no substitute for regular handwashing. The next time you go to a restaurant, look at the kitchen staff's hands.

If they are wearing gloves, look at the state of the gloves. Watch what they touch and what they do while wearing those gloves. If you see cooks and kitchen staff without gloves, that is safer. Hopefully, they are washing their hands and taking the proper precautions required for a clean environment.

Staff Breaks & Habits

Restaurant staff members have to take a break at some point. For those that smoke, this means taking periodic smoke breaks so that they can get the nicotine that they need. The problem with smoke breaks is that they take time, and they encourage non-smoking staff members to also take unnecessary breaks.

If staff members seem to be on a break all the time, there could be a vast number of them that smoke. This is sometimes the case in quiet restaurants. A lone table will sit unattended because all the staff have gone outside for a smoke and have forgotten about the time while deep in their own conversations.

The impression is very, very bad for the customer—who will never come back. A customer should never have to wait for their bill or for service. A poorly-run restaurant means lots of breaks and bad habits. These can range from eating a staff meal in front of customers to wiping their dirty hands on their aprons.

Staff[27] can also get into the bad habit of hanging around their tables too much. This can pester customers into leaving or hurrying through their meal. Being constantly watched makes people feel

---

26 Chris Morran, *Study: Gloves No Substitute for Hand-Washing When It Comes to Food Prep*, http://consumerist.com/2010/10/13/study-gloves-no-substitute-for-hand-washing-when-it-comes-to-food-prep/

27 Lisa McQuerrey, *How to Confront Employees With Disturbing Habits*, http://smallbusiness.chron.com/confront-employees-disturbing-habits-44193.html

uncomfortable. A needy waiter is an irritation and will chase customers away faster than the germs on those condiments.

A few more bad habits that staff members have developed over the years are staring at their phones during service, bringing the bill too early or too late, clearing half-finished food off a table, talking loudly to friends, causing a disruption in the restaurant due to pranks, and being a nuisance to customers instead of a help.

CHAPTER 6
LESSONS FOR THE CUSTOMER

> *"The toughest thing about the power of trust is that it's very difficult to build and very easy to destroy. The essence of trust building is to emphasize the similarities between you and the customer."*
>
> — THOMAS J. WATSON

At this point, you are getting to know the pretty gross things that happen in and around your average restaurant. But there is a whole new stack of problems that step into the mix when a staff member is forced to serve a bad customer.

Customers can and do behave badly—it comes with the territory. That is why I decided to include this delightful segment here—so that you can see if your actions and behaviors are contributing to the unhappiness of servers and kitchen staff all over the U.S.!

Common Courtesy for Staff

It is nice to be nice. Interestingly, most people would insist that they are really nice people. Talk to anyone that has worked as wait staff for a few years and you will quickly learn that the numbers are skewed. Every day, without fail, there is always one customer—or ten depending on how bad the day gets—that decides to treat you like an animal.

Sometimes if you are really unfortunate, you will be publically humiliated and involved in an overblown scene straight from someone's mental health nightmare—and all because you forgot to bring the milk warmed up, which was the trigger they had been waiting for to unleash twenty years' worth of repressed frustration onto you.

Common courtesy is not as common as people like to believe it is. There are dozens of websites online where restaurant staff have gathered to share their outrageous stories about rude, horrible, delusional, and downright shady customers. Customers are people too, and as you know, people can be a handful, especially when alcohol is involved.

As a general rule, you should understand that your server[28] is not there to be your slave. Many are studying to become doctors, lawyers, and your future boss. Even if they are not, they would also like to have a pleasant day at work without a volcano exploding. Common courtesy includes treating people with respect, saying thank you and please, and being patient.

Nothing gives a customer the right to shout at, swear at, or make demands of a staff member. They are there to help you, not pander to your every whim. Some whims deserve to be packed away and never spoken about again. Some are downright ridiculous. Please,

---

28   Matt Walsh, *Maybe You Get Bad Customer Service Because You're a Bad Customer,* http://www.huffingtonpost.com/matt-walsh/bad-customer-service_b_3799574.html

dear reader, have compassion the next time you go out to eat at a restaurant.

Mistreatment of Waiters

The wait staff has to deal directly with the crazies and blatantly rude people that decide to pick their restaurant to grab a bite. I am not talking about you, but perhaps you know a person like this—someone that treats waiters like they do not matter and is dismissive, rude, or short with them because they somehow see themselves as superior.

Then there are the people that love to take out their daily stress on poor restaurant staff, no matter what they do to help. These people channel their marriage, children, and work frustration directly at their waiter for no good reason, other than very bad manners and horrifying disrespect for other human beings.

There are people in the world that manage to make it through their whole lives without having to berate a single waiter! Imagine that. Here are some tips to help you get through service with a smile on your face. It makes for a better experience on both sides.

- Smile and say hello to your server. Too many people just file in, ignoring the waiter completely until they need something. They do not look up but continue chatting to their family and friends, and it makes the waiter feel awkward and disrespected.
- Ask legitimate questions upfront. If you have a concern or want to know the answer to something, then ask. The more direct you are about what you want to know, the easier it becomes to serve you. Not knowing is not an excuse for bad behavior, free food, or a shouting match.
- If you see the staff is distracted, give them a break. It may be a slow day, or they may be dealing with some baggage in their own lives. Wait staff are people too! Have some

compassion, and be forgiving instead of irritated. Things can spiral very quickly when both a server and a customer are in a foul mood.

- If a real problem has occurred that needs to be sorted out—but you are not making any progress with the server—that is the time[29] to call the manager, not when the server is trying to help in every way but you want to have a big rant. You will get everyone in trouble for no good reason.

- Shut your mouth on social media. Consider for a moment that publically shaming a server (on a bad day) or an entire restaurant is unfair and very bad behavior. You are messing with someone's job and an entrepreneur's livelihood—all because you did not get "extra cheese"? Try to calm down before jumping online for a pity-fest.

How to Order Your Food

Ordering food is easy, right? You walk in, sit down, have a quick look through the menu, and choose something that you feel like eating. It is not rocket science. Yet doing this simple act gives a lot of badly-behaved customers trouble. To clarify what should be done, I am going to outline it here, step by step.

First up, grab a menu. If your waiter does not give you a menu shortly after you have been seated, make your way to the front where they are congregated and ask for one. There is no need to be rude; I promise they have forgotten for a good reason. Perhaps the manager was making them do something else more important at the time.

Regardless, they are not ignoring you on purpose. Once you have your menu, it is your job to wade through the various options and pick wisely. If you have any questions, now is the time to ask

---

29 *Customers Behaving Badly: How to Avoid Being One of Them, http:// tiethemoneyknot.com/customers-behaving-badly-how-to-avoid-being-one-of-them/*

them. Once you have organized who will be sitting where, politely tell your server what you want.

Include any allergies or changes to the dish clearly and openly. Be honest; you do not have to pretend like a tomato will kill you just to get it off your plate. Your server will recite the order back to you and hurry off to the kitchen to place that order. You have a five-minute window for any changes after that, but it is not okay to decide that you want something else when the dish has already been cooked.

All raw materials have been used, and the labor has been provided, which means you are liable to pay for it. Always thank your server for their suggestions and when they bring your food or clear your table. Establishing light[30] banter with your server improves their day and your experience. Excellent wait staff members do this automatically, but the shyer among them will need an invitation to relax and enjoy the experience.

Ordering food is about asking the right questions and hearing what your server suggests. You can absolutely mention that you are not looking for the special but that you genuinely feel like a great dish with a certain type of meat in it. The server is more likely to cast aside the upselling and be honest if you do this directly.

If your server at any point forgets an ingredient, makes a mistake, or brings you the wrong thing—give them a break, especially if it is busy. It can be a real challenge balancing 10–15 tables and remembering what everyone wanted. Above all, be cheerful!

How to Pay for Your Meal

There was once a nightmare experience that I heard about from a friend, who was also working as a waitress at the time. A large group of college students walked into the restaurant one evening, rowdy and boisterous as ever.

---

30 Patrick Maguire, *64 Suggestions for Restaurant Customers*, http://www.servernotservant.com/2009/11/05/64-suggestions-for-restaurant-customers/

They all had Groupons, a type of coupon deal that discounts certain food on order. Of course, the fine print said that one Groupon was allowed per table. They sat down and ordered, eating and drinking. When the time came for the bill, they demanded separate checks for ten different couples, hoping to use all of their Groupons.

"Why does it matter where we sit? We all came at the same time," said one drunken student. After a long process of explaining the payment structure and many conversations with angry, drunk students on the part of the waitress and the manager, the kids paid— but they were still a few hundred short, which one kid reluctantly paid on threat of police involvement.

It caused a massive scene in the restaurant and escalated quickly, disturbing other patrons. Scenes like these are thankfully uncommon, but they do happen—especially on Friday and Saturday nights. As a rule, you should always request separate checks upfront as you sit down, before you order.

If you have a coupon[31] deal, check with the wait staff what the rules are because rules there will be. As for tips, the rules on this have not changed in years. For great service, tip extra. For standard service, tip the required percent. For poor service, you can still make the choice to only tip a little or not at all. Tips are not compulsory in small groups.

However, tips are how many wait staff earn their money. You never know if there is a tip pool or if the wait staff have to split their tips with bussers and other staff. Assume that a standard tip is the least you can give, which is what I do. Imagine if you were paid every day according to your mood—would there be days you were paid less? Keep that in mind.

---

31 Caroline Potter, *Diners Behaving Badly: What Annoys You About Other Restaurant Patrons?*, *http://blog.opentable.com/2010/diners-behaving-badly-what-annoys-you-about-other-restaurant-patrons/*

Customers also have no right to demand anything for free if they have ordered it. It is best to express your displeasure by never coming back rather than causing a scene over the salad that cost a dollar. Paying for your meals should be done in full with a full tip— something extra is wonderful if you can afford it.

What to Do When You Need Help
(Hint: Don't Be Rude)

Tone and attitude are everything when dealing with wait staff. Sure, you are going to come across waiters and waitresses that hate their jobs. You might catch them on a bad day, or in a crisis, or under severe stress because they are short staffed.

Whatever the case, keep your tone and attitude in check. Rudeness is a great way to ensure that no one is happy at the end of the experience. It casts suspicion on your food and causes ugly feelings at your table. I have seen many people simply get up and leave after being "insulted" by a dismissive waiter that was busy.

If you want to be a help to your server, then chill out. The job is difficult and stressful enough without being berated over a cream, instead of foam, cappuccino. Of all the jobs in the world, wait staff get the most abuse from random strangers. When you need help, it is best to be friendly, confident, and direct with your approach.

Sitting at a table and seething over lack of service—or a missing fork or a dirty placemat—is not going to help anyone. Get up and find help. That in itself is enough to warrant action on the part of the wait staff. When a customer is direct and honest about things, it is understandable. No one wants that when they dine out!

But a constant negative[32] and aggressive or condescending undertone the next time the server comes to your table is bad behavior. You are not stuck like a magnet to your chair, lording

---

32 *Waiters and Waitresses Reveal the Worst Things a Customer Can Do,* http://magazine.foxnews.com/at-home/waiters-and-waitresses-reveal-worst-things-customer-can-do

over restaurant land. You are a person, and so are they. You can both help each other out. I am not making excuses for the really bad servers among us, but most people are just trying to do their jobs in relative peace and happiness.

- To help your server, do not stack your plates on top of each other or arrange the plates and cutlery in any way. I have worked at multiple places, and there are different systems for each. Most of the time your stack is a massive hindrance and a constant play on the nerves of your habitual server.
- Do not decide on a different table halfway through service. It can and does confuse your server. It is better to find your table at the beginning, while you are being seated. Prefer one at the far end? Great, then speak up now.
- Do not be funny with your tips by leaving suggestions instead of cash. Not only can servers not live off suggestions, but these are universally rude, whether they are meant in jest, as religious inspirations, or as nasty methods of not paying for good service.
- Playing on your cell phone the entire time then suddenly demanding service and complaining about the long wait is rude. I have known many waiters that will not approach a customer because they were taught to wait until they were finished with their phones before taking an order.

The Many Methods of Mistreating Staff

There are a lot of ways people can mistreat the staff at a restaurant. To give you a clearer idea of what not to do, here are some of my personal favorite experiences and some I have heard about along the way.

A drunk woman once misplaced her credit card when it came time for the bill to be paid. Even though everyone helped her search for it, she was convinced the barman stole it. So she called the police. But when they arrived, she approached them so aggressively that she was arrested for public drunkenness.

Sometimes customers will become enraged based on assumptions. One customer did this with a dish he thought contained cilantro in it, an herb he strongly disliked. Even though the herb was Thai basil, the customer refused to believe the waiter, the manager, and the chef, and he refused to pay for his meal—the meal he had eaten more than half of by that time.

Managers are often berated over serving customers with a plate that has become chipped in the dishwasher or a ceramic mug with a hairline crack in it. I have seen people storm out over little more than "second rate" utensils. Staff often get the backlash from the owners' decisions, not just once but multiple times from multiple people.

Adults regularly try to get away with ordering food from the kids' menu, which is a courtesy for their kids. They do not understand that this is possible because of the full meals they will order. Trying to get kids' portions instead is a mistreatment of the restaurant system, which exists to earn money. Arguing about ordering off the kids' menu for adults is extremely rude.

Then there are those people that blow[33] up over nothing. Forgotten food, plates placed in front of the wrong people, incorrect orders, giving the order to the wrong table, or replacing the food with something that tastes worse—none of these things warrants screaming and a scene. First of all, not all of these things are the server's fault.

Sometimes the chef could be having a lazy or bad day. The food quality is not the responsibility of the server, yet they will get all the attitude for it. Patrons have demanded free food due to "doggy bags" they requested that were thrown away by mistake, and they

---

33 *Ruth Chenetz, What Would You Do? Rude Customer Insults Server, http:// abcnews.go.com/WhatWouldYouDo/rude-customer-insults-server/story?id=12638062*

have demanded discounts after contaminating their own food.

While these instances are thankfully not overly common, rudeness is fast becoming a restaurant epidemic. Do not mistreat your server, and you will get better service. It is best to be the kind of person that —if you see the server is having a bad day—makes their lives easier. That is just good karma, and it pays to treat others with respect.

CHAPTER 7

THE PROBLEM WITH ICE BUCKETS

> "Dirt used to be a badge of honor.
> Dirt used to look like work. But we've
> scrubbed the dirt off the face of work, and
> consequently we've created this suspicion
> of anything that's too dirty."
>
> MIKE ROWE

Because I have worked with many teams at a restaurant, I have also seen the nasty reality behind one particular area in the restaurant that has earned its title. Known as the dirtiest places in the restaurant, anywhere the ice goes, germs go with it.

This chapter is about opening your eyes to the torrid world of ice making, storage, use, and abuse that happens in your average restaurant today. The next time you order that glass of wine, it may be better to ignore the ice that comes with it!

The Dirtiest Place in the Restaurant

Have you ever heard of dirty ice? Probably not if you are a humble, unassuming customer that does not see the inner workings of a restaurant very often. Like most customers, you enjoy a lovely glass of wine brimming with shiny ice cubes, or you prefer your soda when the glass is overflowing with ice. There is nothing like a chilled drink, I think you will agree.

At the same time, you are likely to have a friend that hates public restrooms. They are afraid of the germs and freak out over restaurant facilities whenever you go out. This is because public perception dictates that the most germs hang around the bathroom area. Naturally, this perception is untrue.

Ice holds that distinguished title, as recently proven in a study conducted by the Daily Mail.[34] Some six of the ten restaurants they tested had ice cubes that contained dirtier water than the water found in their toilet bowls. Not only is this a food safety risk, but so few people know about it that they never even see the danger coming.

Ice machines are a blight on the restaurant industry. They are misused, never cleaned, and, as a result, become the most bacteria-infested areas in the restaurant. A dirty ice machine can cause illness, food poisoning, and worse to customers with sensitive immune systems and stomachs. Fast food restaurants are the worst, followed by large restaurant chains.

The interior of an ice machine is virtually slathered in germs, which makes dirty ice a real problem. The most potent combination is dirty ice and dirty soda from their respective machines. Whole colonies of bacteria and bugs gravitate towards these areas for water, food, and warmth. They are ideal homes for roaches, mites, bugs, and microscopic germs.

---

34 Hugh Merwin, *Another Study Determines Restaurant Ice Machines Contain More Bacteria Than Toilet Water*, http://www.grubstreet.com/2013/06/ice-machines-bacteria-toilet-water.html

Ice Bucket Attractions Exposed

There you are, sitting across from your loved one and having a romantic evening. You order a bottle of the restaurant's best wine, and it is served to you in an ice bucket. Some people even believe that the ice scoop is there so that you can transfer ice from the ice bucket into your glasses. I have seen them do it despite the bottle in the ice.

First of all, friends, the ice bucket is one of those "shortcut" areas that waiters love to take advantage of during a busy shift. Thanks to the fact that "only ice" has been inside them, they require little more than to be emptied out, right? Good as new! The only problem is that the ice inside the bucket was teaming with bacteria and other creepy crawlies.

Every time an ice bucket is not washed out, the bacteria in that bucket explodes. As a rule, you should never, ever consume ice out of the ice bucket—not because it has touched your "dirty bottle" but because it may contain bar ice. And if you have worked at a bar, you know the difference between bar ice and normal ice.

In a bar, ice[35] is used to chill bottles or may even be used in a large tray where the bartender dips glasses into that ice multiple times. Sometimes these glasses are not clean; they are being reused. So added to your delicious cocktail of bacteria, you also have germs from other people in there—thanks to dipping or use in the bar.

Then there is the fact that ice in an ice bucket is not considered to be ice that will be consumed. So the kitchen staff have no problem touching it, dirty hands and all. Some kitchen staff may even rinse their hands a little in there, seizing on the opportunity to clean off what is on them. You have to be really careful when it comes to the innocent ice bucket.

---

35 *Beth Levine, The Germ-Filled Truth About Restaurants, http://www.grandparents. com/health-and-wellbeing/health/food-borne-illnesses*

To recap, ice buckets are among the most foul of all restaurant items. Not only are they never washed but they contain dirty ice plus bar germs and bacteria from the people that have handled the ice when they were packing it around your bottle. To top that cocktail of filth off, there is the bottle itself, which contains many human hand germs.

The Functions of an Ice Machine

An ice machine sounds like a clean place, but in reality, it can be an atrocious mess. Whenever I start working at a new restaurant, I will check out the ice machine. It is always the grossest, dirtiest thing you can tackle—because it has never been cleaned. If a restaurant has been open for 20 years, that means you have twenty years' worth of germs crawling over you and getting frozen with your water.

Commercial ice machines should be thoroughly cleaned every month. If they are not, a "slime" is created that promotes the growth of bacteria colonies. Worse yet, black mold develops and attracts all kinds of critters that come and live underneath your machine.

Ice is considered a food product by the FDA, which makes you wonder why these machines are not looked after better. The quickest test is to empty the ice out of the machine and do the finger swab test. Black slime is a sign that every single cube is contaminated with the worst kinds of bacteria you could ever imagine.

Ice is a major reason why people get ill at restaurants. They will blame the food they ate, when in actual fact it was a foodborne illness hidden in their ice cubes. Ice machines are used to make restaurant ice, which in turn is used for drinks, food presentation, food storage, in ice buckets, and at the bar.

For restaurants, the ice machine[36] is a necessary expense. So much ice is needed on a daily basis that creating their own is important. Then there are restaurants that buy packaged ice and store them in large bins for the day. These can be just as dirty as the ice machines themselves, and the restaurant can never be sure how that ice was made or handled.

In most cases, the mishandling of ice is to blame for 90% of contaminations. Packaged ice can certainly carry E. coli, salmonella, and many other dangerous bacteria, all because they came into contact with the factory workers' hands. Bacteria reproduces and grows at alarming rates, so you only need a little to contaminate a lot.

Unfortunately, ice is the forgotten food. People do not treat it like a food source and mishandle it because of that. The out of sight, out of mind convenience of these ice machines makes them a restaurant trap. There is a good chance that every beverage you consume that contains ice is also brimming with bacteria.

What Lives in the Ice

Germs survive the freezing process, and other germs make an excellent slime coating on dirty ice. For many years, it was believed that freezing something killed all the micro-organisms that contaminated the water—but recent studies have proven this to be monumentally false. Intestinal upsets will still happen when that ice is consumed!

And if you are relying on your alcohol to nuke whatever microbes are left over, think again. It turns out that freezing the cubes reduces the bacteria but does not kill them all. An ice cube only needs to be highly contaminated in order for it to cause an intestinal upset. The freezing process especially creates a mildly reduced cube of bacteria for you to drink.

36 *Does a Killer Live Inside Your Dirty Ice Machine?*, *http://tekexpressny.com/dirty-ice#.VZpj0vmqpBc*

Experts are even advising travelers to steer clear of ice from other countries because of these trapped microbes. While your body may be strong enough to handle most bacteria forms in your own country, step outside, and any new forms will cause an upset. As a rule, when traveling to far-flung locations, avoid ice like it carries the plague.

When someone asks you why you are avoiding ice, tell them that the freezing process reduces the germs but does not kill them. With ice's ability to be neglected as a food source, it is already more contaminated than many other things you will put in your body.

Some of the wild and wacky bacteria[37] found in ice include coliform bacteria, mold, E. coli, salmonella, human feces, human mucus, and even deadly viruses. While these viruses have been known to be transmitted in ice, thankfully it does not happen often. This is due to the government regulating and setting standards for creating ice in the industry.

What lives in your favorite restaurant's ice is all down to their practices and level of hygiene. I have seen some of the cleanest restaurants neglect their ice machine, while fairly average restaurants take great care to keep their ice super clean. It depends on the owner and staff and the practices they have in place.

The most important thing to remember is that freezing water does not automatically kill all bacteria. Likewise, touching something frozen does not kill germs on contact. Ice is not some magical thing that is immune to dirt and germs. On the contrary, due to its watery nature and the fact that it is used for so many dishes and drinks, it is a danger for everyone involved.

What Happens to the Ice

Restaurant ice machines come in all shapes and sizes. Truly, you never know where your ice is coming from when you step into a

---

37 Todd Van Luling, *3 Gross Things You Didn't Know Were in Your Ice Cubes*, http://www.huffingtonpost.com/2014/06/16/ice-cubes-gross_n_5475301.html

new restaurant. The larger ice machines can make up to 30 pounds of ice a day, all in a matter of 15 minutes. For the busy restaurant, this process is essential, but it also means a lot of work, water, and washing.

Most people are convinced that ice machines are naturally cold, so it is impossible for any germs and bacteria to grow in there. How wrong they are! The ice machine itself is almost always warm, which makes it an excellent habitat for roaches and other creepy crawlies that like to infest warm, damp places.

During everyday use, the ice gets progressively dirty by many different means. Gross, food-encrusted or drink-splashed hands regularly dip inside the ice machine, spreading human germs in the existing ice and even in the water section. If the water is not changed frequently enough at slow restaurants, it can become a bacteria soup primed for freezing.

Older ice[38] can contaminate new ice, or the machine can be left to create cubes over and over again without ever being cleaned. This is the most common way machines become a germ wasteland—non-cleaning. The insides of the machine quickly become slimy and black thanks to mold and human germs that contaminate the surroundings.

This dirty water freezes, melts, and can be refrozen again and again from the machine, causing numerous issues for the ice cubes being created. It is so important to clean that ice machine thoroughly at least once a month, although twice is better for adequate hygiene.

The plastic tubing in the ice machines can also become clogged, which traps bacteria and ensures that all consecutive batches of ice are spoiled. The trick is that you cannot see contaminated ice; it is completely transparent and microscopic, so you never know what

---

38 *Dirty Ice Makers Will Get You Sick, http://www.newair.com/articles/dirty-ice-makers-will-get-you-sick/*

you are putting in your drinks. A bad taste is the biggest clue that something is not right with the ice.

A University of Texas study[39] found that ice cubes contain salmonella, E. coli, and shigella even when mixed with hard liquor, soda, and water. Dirty ice can make people extremely ill, either by planting germs that become flu or other illness or by giving them gastrointestinal problems, food poisoning, and headaches. Best to keep track of where your ice comes from.

Decisions About Ice

How do you go about protecting yourself from this widespread risk of contaminated ice machines and cubes in your local restaurant? The only thing you can do is talk to the manager about their cleaning practices or decide not to have any ice in your drink. As a rule, when I am at a bar, I will never have ice in anything.

This ensures that I do not pick up the maximum amount of bacteria the restaurant has to offer simply by having a soda or an average drink with ice in it. Call your waiter over, and ask them how often they clean their ice machine. If they do not know the answer, this is a red flag. All staff should automatically know the answer.

Preceding that question with "How long have you worked here?" will give you a better impression of the landscape. If they have been working at that restaurant for two years but have no clue about ice machine cleaning practices, that is a red flag. Typically, if the answer is not instantly "twice a month or at least once," I do not go near their ice.

If no one is around to ask, I avoid it for the reasons I have given. Ice is not to be messed around with. Even ice that has come from packages or bags supplied by an ice manufacturer can be contaminated, although the chances are less likely. While you can risk drinking these ice cubes, a restaurant's open ice that they make

---

39 *Newair, Dirty Ice Makers Will Get You Sick. <http://www.newair.com/articles/ dirty-ice-makers-will-get-you-sick/>*

themselves is questionable.

Personally, I would rather ask the question and avoid a few evenings of lavatory duty than assume the ice is okay—only to get home and realize I was wrong. When you know this about the ice machine, you cannot pretend not to know it. And that hard fact is that most restaurants fail to clean their machine regularly enough, if at all.

Germs[40] survive the freezing process, and the ice picks up more germs along the way from negligent practices. Those are indisputable facts. So the question you need to ask yourself is— should I risk it? Better to not have any ice at a dodgy-looking restaurant. If you are feeling brave and the restaurant seems to be very clean, go ahead.

In the same breath, if you have been on antibiotics or have a weakened immune system for any reason, avoid the ice. It will make you sick. Even small traces of that bacteria will cause a storm in your system when your defenses are lowered.

Do you know why when you go out for a night on the town you feel flu-like for a week after hitting it hard? It was not the liquor; it was the ice in the liquor. You drank several glasses of it, and that bacteria enjoyed the opportunity to make you ill the next day. It is time to invest in a neat glass of something you do not mind as a room temperature alternative.

40 *Karl Neumann, M.D., Hold The Ice: Germs Survive Freezing, Alcohol, http:// articles.chicagotribune.com/1989-08-13/travel/8901040291_1_ice-cubes-drink-bacterial-count*

CHAPTER 8
SPECIALS & PROMOTIONS

> *"We are all in the business of sales.*
> *Teachers sell students on learning, parents*
> *sell their children on making good grades*
> *and behaving, and traditional salesmen*
> *sell their products."*
>
> DAVE RAMSEY

There are some restaurants that exist in the U.S. that practice a slew of suspicious behaviors regarding how they choose to use their "specials" board. The reality is that a great restaurant might use specials as the customer perceives them to, while average and badly-run restaurants do not.

Promoting food has instead become a reason to push profit margins, to get rid of old food quickly, to move too much product, and to sell a specialty item made from leftover dishes. The truth behind some of these practices would make your hair stand on end!

How Do Specials Come About?

My husband and I once went on vacation to a lovely island retreat, where we rented a small, two-room house that was about 200 square feet in size. The house had a tin roof and was atop one of the most gorgeous hills I had ever laid eyes on.

We used water from a huge bucket outside, which was also our makeshift kitchen. There was no refrigeration or electricity—a true island getaway. We had access to a little outhouse, so we were roughing it in the truest sense.

After we had freshened up, four of us went down to the beach for dinner at sunset. We chose sandwiches from the concession stand, a safe bet. Then we retired back to the house to enjoy our beautiful surroundings. The next morning we headed down to the resort to grab some breakfast and discovered Momma's Store, a downtown area for the locals.

The store appeared to be clean and bright except for her special cakes, which were crawling with roaches. Behind Momma's were about a dozen shacks with one community water tap. A man stood outside chopping raw chicken to sell on the street. No refrigeration, no sanitation, and no hygiene there. Tourists just loved Momma's local specials.

For the average restaurateur like Momma, a special is something reserved for moving stock or solving a business problem more than it is a treat for the customer. Special promotions help keep the business open, which is why they should be viewed with suspicion.

Food Poisoning: Bisque Anyone?

I have a history with a New England-style lobster bisque that contained large chunks of "fresh" lobster. Both times this "delicious" bisque was promoted as a restaurant special, a favorite, and a crowd pleaser. Some restaurants love to feed you lies along with your main course, and in this case, I was nothing more than a target.

You know food poisoning the first time it hits you. It is not like other illnesses at all. Your entire body begins to revolt against the hideous fuel you poured into it, and it lunges into overdrive to get it out as soon as possible. The onset happens about 4–12 hours after eating or drinking something bad. Unfortunately, the illness can last that long as well.

You become a slave to your retching body and a permanent resident of the bathroom for the next 10 hours at least. That is what happens when a restaurant chef abuses what should be a customer "special." In your mind, you believe the promotion has happened because the chef discovered some great, affordable lobster at the local fish market.

You imagine that this lobster bisque was lovingly planned out by a passionate chef that wants to keep customers flowing through their restaurant. After all, a special is supposed to be, well, special, isn't it? Alas, this was not the case for me that day. Or the second time. On both occasions, I was fooled by the marketing promotions of a restaurant.

What I suspect really happened was that the chef decided to use some lobster that was reaching the end of its shelf life by disguising the turning product in a highly seasoned soup to disguise any bad taste. Bisque can be delicious when made with fresh ingredients, but—rather insidiously—it can also be used to mask that "off" flavor crustaceans have when they have become too old to eat.

These "not-so" specials[41] are designed to use up the rest of what is essentially old, rotting product so that the chef has something to sell without losing profit on inventory and sales. It is diabolical, especially when this bad practice often results in food poisoning for their patrons. My advice would be to stay away from "specials" disguised in additional flavors.

---

41   *The 5 Secrets Restaurants Don't Want You to Know, http://www.doctoroz.com/ article/5-secrets-restaurants-dont-want-you-know*

Typically, you are safer if you steer clear of the three S's: spaghetti, soup, and sauce. A chowder, stew, bisque, or pasta is a great way to disguise foul-tasting meat or produce.

What Lurks in the Soup

While many chefs do place legitimately fresh produce on their specials menu, this is not the case for the average restaurant. Sadly, many places fall into bad habits when it comes to pushing product, moving old food, and getting money in before it is too late.

You have to be suspicious of what lurks in that special soup. Anything, in fact, that comes slathered in sauce could be a trick to mask a bad flavor. You should pick wisely off the specials menu, and never ask for food drowning in saucy herbs. This is how you can enjoy a lunch that chains you to a bathroom for the next two days.

Shellfish specials are particularly suspect, as I discovered the hard way. Anything from mussels, fish, and lobster to your basic shrimp can be funky. I have been poisoned[42] by fried flounder and draft beer. One time a waitress noticed I was put off by a bad-smelling shrimp dish, which she promptly removed. My dinner guest ate his and vomited all night long.

The worst restaurant I ever worked in used soups in particular to disguise scraps of food that were too old to use anywhere else. The "soup du jour" or soup of the week can be a hazard to your health. Not only are there old items of food in there, but handling can make things worse. Temperatures, cooling, and storage can all result in a properly rotten dish.

Soups are often canned or bagged, which is fine, but a handmade soup means that old, rotting veggies and other bits were blended and converted into your soup of the day. These can contain mold, E. coli and other bacteria from the rotting process. Pushing

---

42 William Blahd, M.D., *Food Poisoning*, http://www.webmd.com/food-recipes/food-poisoning/food-poisoning

something that is about to go bad can happen for days after the dish has gone bad!

I really have seen it all, and it has made me very suspicious of restaurant specials. Sometimes the chef will be having a lazy day, so they will want to whip something up that is quick and easy. This is fine because the produce is fresh. But I have seen chefs pick laziness and then randomly charge more than the listed menu price for these dishes! Buyer beware indeed. Never trust a restaurant special that does not feel right.

What Goes in the Fryer Stays in the Fryer

Another interesting risk to your health and wellbeing comes from bad practices surrounding the fryer. Oil is an expensive commodity and one that is reused many times in a restaurant. The horrifying bit comes in when you realize that the oil is rarely changed.

What this means is that all foods that are being deep fried in that fryolater are mixing together—which could invoke some pretty serious allergic reactions in people with sensitivities. While the deep frying action does tend to kill most bacteria, this does not make the fryer an ally in your fight against eating old food.

In fact, chefs will often take old chicken and beef products and deep fry them because it rids them of a smell and kills off most of the festering bacteria. You will be eating rotten meat, and you may never know it. Food poisoning happens at different levels. It can be violent, or it can be a general feeling of illness that upsets your stomach a little, but you are not sure why.

If you have eaten some kind of blended special, like chicken and spaghetti, it is because these deep fried items were old and rotting already. I have worked in many excellent restaurants that neglect safe frying practices. They fry shrimp and seafood in the fryer, and then they will deep fry someone's chicken in it, regardless of whether or not they have a deathly reaction to shellfish.

Oil is badly handled in a lot of places, and that means failure to change the oil often enough as well. Week-old oil that gently smokes as you use it is downright poisonous, and it taints the flavor of everything that is added to it. If your fried food tastes of old oil, send it back! It means that your chef has iffy oil-changing practices and needs to sort it out.

The best way to see if oil can be reused is its color. If the color is off, the oil is overused. Black oil[43] is the worst because it has been used so many times. Cleaning a fryer is a long and arduous job that takes time and effort. People are not excited to do it, and so it does not get done as often as it should be done. I would personally stay away from deep fried anything.

Questions to Ask Your Waiter

There are many reasons why you should have a good relationship with your waiter. First of all, they know about all of these heinous practices and will be less likely to serve you old food if you outright ask them the right questions—without being rude.

This is particularly true when it comes to seafood. There is a joke in the restaurant business when a customer asks about the seafood. "Is the seafood fresh?" they will say. "Does it come from the Gulf?" In the waiter's mind, they are thinking, "Yeah, the Persian Gulf," but they will nod their head in agreement, knowing full well the seafood is fresh-frozen.

There are very few restaurants that serve local seafood, and the majority of them choose to use frozen items for longevity and sales. This seafood comes in frozen from China or another distant place halfway across the world. It is bought because it is cheap and the restaurant owner wants to improve their profit margins.

---

43 Jason Rahm, *Restaurant Hazards Posed by Commercial Fryers*, *http://www. foodservicewarehouse.com/education/product-safety-public-health/restaurant-hazards-posed-by-commercial-fryers/c28213.aspx*

Ask them if they freeze their seafood or if their seafood is frozen. This is a more direct question than "Is it fresh?" because that invites a lie. I have seen so many bad practices with seafood. I have spotted frozen shrimp or single packaged tuna left in a bucket or in the sink with water running over it to help it defrost.

Even worse are the startling lack of sinks in these restaurants. You have to wash your hands over this food and dump out other food directly next to this food as it is defrosting. That is far from sanitary and quite gross. Waiters lie for a lot of different reasons but mainly because of pressure from their manager or boss.

Occasionally they will lie[44] for a tip, saying whatever the customer wants to hear while pushing the most expensive item on the menu. Waiters do this because they want a larger tip at the end of your bill—be aware of that. Sometimes waiters lie because it is impossible to find something out. The prep team is gone from breakfast, and no one remains.

The chef and shift supervisor often do not know what goes into the soup the prep team made that morning. Ingredient lists get lost, and people become misinformed. Even labeled boxes end up being wrong. Plus, there is fierce competition with other restaurants. If we do not tell you the fish is fresh, you will go across the street where they will lie to you about it.

Free Plated Extras: Warning!

Have you ever heard the saying that there is no such thing as a free meal? This is very true when it comes to restaurant extras! I want to take a moment to warn you about those fun little extras that you get when you go to a nice restaurant.

I have worked in a lot of nice places, where you would never suspect in a million years that kitchen staff are doing what they do.

---

44 *Jenn Abelson, Beth Daley, On the Menu, but Not on Your Plate, http://www.boston. com/business/articles/2011/10/23/on_the_menu_but_not_on_your_plate/*

Free plated extras[45] cost the restaurant a lot of money, so they do everything they can to save on produce and conserve stock. This means that they employ bad practices to save as much of these free extras as they can.

Those open butter dishes that come with your complimentary bread? You may only use a scraping of them, but they are quickly plugged with fresh butter and re-chilled in the kitchen—along with all of your knife and finger bacteria. The butter on the bottom is old, while the fresh butter lingers on top. Rolls and breads are swapped in baskets and make it onto the plates of whoever dares to eat them.

They could have been sneezed on at someone else's table for all you know. Then there are the complimentary vegetables! If it seems like you did not enjoy yours, they are simply added back to the great big vat of them in the kitchen. No point wasting them—after all, they are free! The problem, of course, is that they now contain loads of bacteria.

When this is a practice, a single vat of vegetables can contain ridiculous amounts of bacteria from multiple tables over a period of a few days. You are essentially then being served other people's germs and not complimentary vegetables. This is why I am always suspicious of free plated extras—because they can become caught in "reuse" cycles.

These reuse cycles tend to attract the possibility of contracting illness, food poisoning, and other germs at a much higher rate than normal foods. The same goes for complimentary ice, although this usually melts and is added to a slop bucket or drain if it is not consumed, so no worries about reuse there!

---

45 Stefanie Tuder, 10 Things Restaurants Won't Tell You, http://abcnews.go.com/blogs/lifestyle/2013/12/10-things-restaurants-wont-tell-you/

The Best Time to Eat Out

If you want to optimize your dinner time, then you have to know when the best time is to eat out. This will increase your chance of getting good service and fresh food and finding a restaurant that has better practices than most.

I generally steer clear of brand new restaurants. They can be very hectic, and in my experience, they cut a lot of corners and make a lot of mistakes in the beginning. This can cause all sorts of problems for the customer, so it is best to wait until they have been open for a few months and have sorted through the kinks of their business model.

I also make a point of never going to a restaurant that is closing down. This type of place will make you sick and will do anything to get a buck out of you, which is never a good thing. They are not staying open, so there is nothing to lose by serving you old produce, giving you bad service, and manipulating you according to their needs.

The same can be said for restaurants that are on their way out. They usually only have a quarter of their menu available because they are broke. When I come across these places, I will order a beer and then make up an excuse to leave. Sometimes I will not even bother to order a beer and will simply say that I have forgotten my wallet.

Restaurants that go out of business usually do so because of bad practices, and the last thing that you want is a bad practice restaurant in the month they are closing shop. New restaurants are fun, but they get a lot wrong in the beginning, which can be frustrating for the customer. When a restaurant runs out of too many things, it is usually a very bad sign.

Either there is no money to support the place or someone forgot to do their job. Both of these reasons are strong enough for you to make a fast exit. You just never know what corners are being cut! The best times to eat out are general days, not weekends, holidays,[46] or when the restaurant is at their busiest.

Opening and closing times are a bad choice because staff will be gearing up or down, and they will be half asleep. Shortcuts are taken for these reasons, which can impact the service quality and what you get on your plate.

The Bacteria Buffet

Buffets are all the rage these days because they come with perceived value. But as I was saying earlier, if a restaurant cannot win, they will not bother to serve you that food. Buffets are actually an industry secret for the average restaurant.

Sunday buffets are especially suspicious because it benefits the restaurant so well. They usually order in a bunch of produce for the weekend, and what they do not sell they will convert into buffet foods for consumption on Sunday. Along with this food are all the other foods that are nearing or past their expiration date.

This is a great way the restaurant[47] can save on lost produce while maximizing sales. The old "all-you-can-eat" buffet is even more tempting for the customer, but watch out! Many buffet foods are steeped in spicy or herb-laden sauces and stews. The reason these appear on the buffet table is because they hide older-tasting meats.

I love to eat at a local buffet restaurant every week; it is one of my favorite places to go right now. I am, however, always aware that buffet food can be food poisoning disguised as a yummy soup or stew. I tend to avoid those food items and go for the plainer ones near the back. This is for a few other reasons I discovered while working at a buffet restaurant.

---

46 *A Former Maitre D' Explains Why You Should Stay Home on Valentine's Day,* *http://www.thekitchn.com/a-former-maitred-explains-why-you-should-stay-home-on-valentines-215854*

47 *4 Reasons to Avoid the "All You Can Eat" Buffet, http://www.thealternativedaily. com/4-reasons-avoid-can-eat-buffet/*

Some people love to stand around the table and eat over the food! Waiters are constantly having to shoo people away as they drip bacteria from their own mouths and plates back into the dish other customers will use. I have seen many people neglect the tongs and simply grab a few quick items with their fingers, contaminating the rest of the table.

Plus, there are other hidden dangers, including not knowing what is inside each dish. If you have allergies or are avoiding certain foods, you have to understand that a buffet will contain things you should not be eating. Asking staff may lead to trouble.

Finally, many buffets are chemical and preservative laden, which means that they will contain MSG, trans fats, and other unwanted food enhancers that will keep you coming back for more. It may be delicious, but is that because of the MSG or because the food is genuinely fresh? Do not be encouraged to overeat or gorge on old food.

What Not to Eat at a Bar

CHAPTER 9
BAR PRACTICES TO EMBRACE

> *"After the first glass, you see things as you wish they were. After the second, you see things as they are not. Finally, you see things as they really are, and that is the most horrible thing in the world."*
>
> OSCAR WILDE

Everyone loves to discover a new bar, where you can hang out with your friends and have a good evening of laughter, fun, and interesting drinks. Having a few drinks down at a bar has been a key American pastime since 1673,[48] when the first bars opened in Rhode Island.

In this chapter, I want to impart some important knowledge that you may not have in your street smarts arsenal. It concerns finding and enjoying new bars and the food and drinks that they serve. You have to be savvy if you want to make it out alive!

---

48   Matt Meltzer, *The Oldest Bar in Every State (and DC!)*, http://www.thrillist.com/travel/nation/america-s-oldest-bars-the-oldest-bar-in-all-50-us-states-and-washington-dc

Choosing Frequency Over Taste

You have just discovered this quaint little bar close to your work, so you have decided to go there with some friends on Wednesday for a bite and a beer. You arrive on a chilly evening at 6 p.m. and are seated across from the bar at a fine wooden table.

The waiter wanders over to you and asks for your order. What do you order? You have never been to this bar before. You have no idea what sort of drinks they serve or what the food is like. The place looks decent enough, although like most bars, there could be a lot lurking amidst the dark surroundings and blaring '80s music.

This is the choice that we all have to face when entering a new bar for the first time. You do not know the people or what the quality of food is like, so you rely heavily on your waiter. It is best at this point, at least for the first visit, to employ the frequency over taste rule. This rule states that you should not order what you usually would.

Instead, you should order what seems to be popular to guarantee a better experience and fewer problems for your tummy. Any item on the menu that they are known for is a good idea, along with closed bottle service. It does not matter if you feel like a draft beer this time; those pipes could be savagely dirty—you just do not know.

Tea and Coffee Practices

Going to a bar is inevitably followed by a tea or coffee experience. Bars love to serve caffeinated products, which helps stimulate their clientele and makes them order more food or alcohol over time.

You have to hope that you are getting your coffee from a commercial machine and not a home machine. Home coffee machines are notorious for hiding black mold in them that you then drink when you consume your coffee. Then you have to hope that this machine is cleaned out regularly. This can get really bad at a bar, where heat and moisture are common. Likewise, if that commercial coffee machine is rarely cleaned, you can also experience mold, bacteria, and slime buildup, which you then drink with your caffeine.

A bar can be a really unhygienic[49] place, especially if staff believe that using the machine naturally cleans it out. Asking for specialty things like specific types of chemical-free decaf, skim milk, whole milk, or half and half are impossible. Bar staff will nod while not caring that your request is legitimate and serious to you.

For this reason, you should check how the bar makes their coffee and try to spot where their milk comes from. Do not request anything outside of the normal coffee and milk, or you probably will not get it anyway. I have chatted to bar staff that lie relentlessly to customers just to make those sales.

Cutlery Cleaning 101

The last thing you want to hear about at a bar is how they clean their cutlery because it can be gross. I have worked in many bars during the course of my hospitality career, and I have seen it all, including bars that allow bar staff to "dip" cutlery so that it is superficially clean.

The dipping method is little better than licking the spoon, tongs, or fork in question. It happens because there is usually a readily available pair of bar sinks designed just for glasses, which can act as a fast way of cleaning other things during the course of a busy evening.

To top it off, the freshly-dipped bacteria spoon is then buffed with the bar rag, which contains countless germs, pest residue, and human fecal matter. Bars are generally not very clean places unless you are in a place like a hotel bar. Privately-owned bars

---

49 *Andrew Easthope, Coffee Machine Cleaning Tips, http://www.fivesenses.com.au/ blog/2013/11/05/coffee-machine-cleaning-tips*

have a vast array of problems when it comes to cutlery and the cleaning process.

Some bartenders will even dip in plain view of the customer, as if that behavior is perfectly normal. They have no idea they are contaminating the spoon for the next person and the one after that. The only way you can be sure that cutlery in a bar is clean is if it comes to the table clean. Even then I would check that it has not been improperly washed. Many bars do not use dishwashers because of the sheer volume of glasses that always need to be washed and rotated.

As a rule, I always carry along some antibacterial wet wipes, which I use to clean off any cutlery that I will use in the bar. These implements go directly into your mouth, so there is no messing around when it comes to germ exposure.

If the cutlery has a mild metal smell, the establishment could also be using a silver polish,[50] which can be harmful to your health. It is better to pick up a napkin and wipe the cutlery for safety reasons. If you see black on it, it has been chemically polished. If there is food residue, it has been cleaned badly. Either way, you save yourself a germ invasion!

Customer Access Concerns

Lack of basic hygiene is a real problem for a lot of bars in America. Due to the very nature of a pub, people are in and out of the place, bringing with them a huge variety of stupid, unhygienic behaviors that impact the health and safety of the place.

Drunk people tend to touch more things with reckless abandon, they do not hold their hands up when they sneeze, they vomit on pub furniture or in the bathrooms, and worse. The problem with most bars is that the customer cannot access the kitchen at all.

---

50 Alexandra Duron, *Restaurant Silverware Can Cause Illness*, http://www. prevention.com/health/healthy-living/restaurant-silverware-can-cause-illness

Anything could be happening there, which is an ongoing concern for people like me.

This is especially true when the owner and staff of the bar are allowed to drink, which often happens. While not technically good business, this does nothing to instill faith in the cautious patron. A drunk bartender is more likely to make hygiene mistakes, spill, attract pests, not clean up after themselves, and not care about washing out cloths or things like that.

Then there are all the people! Bars are often overstuffed with patrons vying for a drink, which makes the state of the bathrooms terrible and the chances of you getting a hygienic drink or plate of food minimal. You might be thinking, "Gosh, this is a lot to complain about," and I would agree with you, except that food poisoning has changed my mind on what is and is not acceptable.

A customer should be able to go to the bathrooms when they need to. They should be able to check in to see the kitchens if they want to. Heck, they should be able to inspect every practice in a place if it makes them more comfortable. Technically, training your staff in correct food handling practices is the law,[51] for all of our safety.

Yet I often wonder when I am sitting in a new bar watching the bartender dip a customer's used glass into the ice over and over again—where have the standards gone? Bars have access concerns because they are just not as clean as restaurants, and that is the truth.

Bars That Are Closing Down

A bar that is closing down will have the same or similar problems to a restaurant that is suffering from a financial shortage. Their food will be substandard and so will their drinks. They will do whatever

---

51 *Fact Sheets & Presentations, http://www.fda.gov/Food/GuidanceRegulation/FSMA/ ucm247546.htm*

it takes to get as much money in and product out before close as they can, and this is where the danger comes in.

Because bars are dirtier—and tend to be shrouded in drunken decisions—there is no relying on a bar to serve you what you ask for during that last month of being open. They will lie relentlessly about everything just to sell it. I know because I have gone to a bar that was closing down and saw the carnage taking place.

Staff were no longer cleaning correctly, so the sticky bar became even stickier. Things had vanished or gone missing. Food was flying out of the kitchen poorly cooked, even chicken dishes, which is extremely dangerous. Certain menu items were not available, and there was no longer any effort to change the bar snacks or put out fresh peanuts.

Going to a bar that is closing down[52] might seem like a good idea for "cheap drinks," but in reality, the bar is searching for people to dump a whole lot of old product on. You will be lucky to still find the drinks you enjoy there. Instead, you are more likely to find a vat of the most disgusting "house" brandy or whiskey ever made, selling for $4 doubles.

This means a lot of drunk, unruly people and inevitable fighting. Whenever there are low, low drink specials, there is fighting. A bar that is closing down would love to claim damages from insurance by making their customers extra drunk from cheap drinks. Sometimes they can collect more from the insurance than their own sold stock.

As a rule, I would not eat anything at a bar that is closing down. Stick to closed, bottled drinks, and steer clear of shots—these will be where you pick up the most germs. Like a restaurant, never go for the drinks specials or food specials without understanding why they are special. Are they special for the bar or for you? There is a very big difference!

---

52   Ted Cox, *Problem Bars Could Be Closed by Top Cop Under Proposed New Ordinance, http://www.dnainfo.com/chicago/20150323/downtown/problem-bars-could-be-closed-by-top-cop-under-proposed-new-ordinance*

Recognizing a Taste Issue

While there are some bars in the USA that do incredible food, many do not have a clue about food or cooking it. Owning and running a bar is not the same as running a restaurant. People get into bars for different reasons than they get into opening a restaurant.

Always order clean, popular items that you know a place can do well. Leave the soups, sauces, and stews alone. Instead, go for the burger or pizza option, which is hard to mess up because it is such a classic choice. Your chances of the produce being fresh are higher.

Interestingly, smell is not a good indicator of off or spoiled food. If your dish has a funky smell, it means that it is highly poisonous and may put you in the hospital. The "sniff test" does not work in most restaurants, as bacteria can be odorless or disguised in the smells from other herbs and flavors.

When food spoils,[53] the bacteria have taken over, and this causes a strong smell. But these bacteria are not the same as the ones that cause food poisoning. Even the "taste" test is no sure way of detecting the bacteria that causes food poisoning in a bar.

That said, if you do have a bad smell or taste, send the food back immediately. The chances of you getting ill from that dish are much higher in a bar. At a restaurant, you may consume old product and not get sick, but at a bar, the chances are not in your favor.

Bars are usually muggy and warm, an ideal environment for the spread of bacteria that cause food poisoning issues. So at a bar especially—if your food tastes or smells weird, do yourself a favor and spit it out.

Grab the waiter and send the food back, but be honest. Do not insult the waiter, because it is not their fault. At the same time, do mention that the food is off. Remember a bar is much more likely to be riddled with bacteria because of the nature of what happens there!

---

53 *Can You Smell if Food Is Off?*, *http://www.abc.net.au/health/talkinghealth/factbuster/stories/2014/12/11/4146849.htm*

CHAPTER 10
BAR FOODS TO AVOID

> "Not all chemicals are bad. Without chemicals such as hydrogen and oxygen, for example, there would be no way to make water, a vital ingredient in beer."
>
> —————— DAVE BARRY ——————

There is nothing nicer than sitting back in a comfortable chair at the bar and deciding that you want to nibble on something or perhaps just feast on something fresh inside your next cocktail. However you like to play it, not all bar food is as clean or hygienic as you would like.

In this chapter, I am going to take you through the hazards of eating bar food willy-nilly because you believe it is safe. Guess what—a lot of it is not safe! These are the bar foods that you diligently need to avoid on your next bar run.

The Bar Snack Reality

Traditionally, there are bar snacks, meaning the free food that is put out for you to enjoy with your drinks, and the snack bar, which can be a number of easy-to-access items that are sold behind the bar itself. For the sake of this section, I am going to speak about the open foods, the ones that the bartender lovingly opens and feasts on himself throughout the night.

Bar snacks are gross, and I say this with a certain disdain for the way that people treat them. I have been a bartender before and have seen what people do with these innocent, unassuming foods when you are going about your average evening. First of all, the snacks that are usually put out are peanuts, raisins, popcorn, chips, or chili-based snacks. They are meant to create thirst in the drinker, who will then want to order more to drink. It is an old trick to keep salty, chili-based, and savory snacks around a bar because it works and people like it. People also like to scratch around in these open air snacks. They eat them, pick them up, play with them, and put them back.

Bar snacks[54] are notoriously unsafe areas to eat from, regardless of how clean the bar might be. Frequent bathroom trips mean that bowl has more fecal matter than anyone should be willing to eat. Avoid the tummy rush by avoiding the temptation.

Fruits Slices for Your Drinks

Sometimes a fruity cocktail can make even the worst days seem like paradise. That is why when you are out on the town, drinking at your favorite bar, you would never suspect the hidden danger lurking in your Pina Colada.

Fruit cut behind the bar, on the fly, is nearly always done with unclean hands. These hands have been touching money,

---

54 *Marielaina Perrone DDS, Share: The Dirty Dozen – Dirtiest Items We Place in Our Mouths, http://www.empowher.com/community/share/dirty-dozen-dirtiest-items-we-place-our-mouths*

bottles, glasses, dirty cloths, and customers. The extent of this unsanitary environment differs from bar to bar, but here is what sometimes happens.

The bartender is nearly always the person responsible for cutting this delicious fruit, which they often do in advance. The fruit is then stored for several days and used directly from the fridge. Many times the entire plate of fruit is taken out of the fridge and offered to people doing shots, especially in the case of lemon and orange wedges.

This fruit[55] is almost never rotated, which means that if you get a cocktail with a funky-looking, dried up slice in it, it has been around. Things like olives, cherries, oranges, limes, and lemons are usually stored together, which means cross contamination. You were not imagining it when your cherry tasted like olive juice; it was probably lying in it. These fruit trays are rarely covered for the evening and are left open in the fridge. Flies and other pests often breed in fruit trays in outdoor bars.

Fingers dip into cherry pots all the time, so that tasty cherry comes with added human bacteria. My advice would be to never consume, suck, or enjoy any bar fruit that is hung off your glass or placed inside it. Like lemon wedges, these fruit items are soaked in germs and are not fit for consumption.

Bar Specials Beware

Have you ever gone to a bar just because you heard the specials were so good? For the most part, bar specials are a great way to get the customer through the door. There are some bars that like to exploit this fact, and they will engineer specials to pull people in, get them very drunk, and hope that they return.

The problem with this type of special is that it usually involved very cheap, very bad-for-you alcohol. This sub-par alcohol is

---

55   *Don't Fruit the Beer, http://bartenderdiary.blogspot.com/2010/07/dont-fruit-beer.html*

extremely high in alcohol content and tastes awful. Bar specials are run for "double brandies and Coke" for just a few dollars, when in actual fact, the brandy is the worst, cheapest, most horrible alcohol the owner could find. Drunk people do not know the difference, they say. And if they do, they simply will not order another one.

Chips, Salsa & Condiments

In the bar industry, there is an unspoken rule that many practice. It is called the "never double dip" rule, and it pertains to the chip and dip areas in a bar. Sometimes a nice bar will offer their customers some complimentary chip and dip. Yum! There is no better way to get your appetite working and build up a hunger.

Unfortunately, as with anything in a bar, you never quite know what happens to the food that is open for public consumption! Even the condiments are not safe. A friend of mine once came back after putting out some chip and dip in a busy bar and found all the chips ground to a powder, leaking with dip, with all of the surrounding condiments poured on top of it.

What could she say? Drunk people do stupid things, and when you put food out, a drunk person may get a hold of it. For the less drunk people that are only congregating, drinking, and behaving, the chip and dip area is something to fight over. Courteously, they will wait their turn for a chip and a dip. Then they will double dip.

Double dipping[56] is when you dip your clean chip, bite it, and dip it again so that your mouth bacteria infects the rest of the dip for everyone else. While this only allows a small amount of bacteria into the dip, bacteria from multiple mouths adds up quickly.

And a word of warning for everyone that uses condiments at a busy bar. The condiments are also available to the public, which means drunk people can and will get a hold of them. They love to add salt, different sauces, bits of paper, and alcohol to the

---

56 *Double-Dipping – Explain It to Me, http://chowhound.chow.com/topics/768856*

condiments. This seems to give a lot of people a very happy time, but sadly, it ruins the sauce for everyone else.

I do not know how many times I had to throw salt, sauce, and other condiments away because drunk people decided to play with them. Be careful of consuming these as they come from a public place brimming with hilarious people. Better to use sealed packets just in case, which is what I always do.

Better Choices for Foods

Bar food can be some of the most tasty, spicy, and delicious food that you can get in your town. Yet because of the nature of bars as a whole, you should decide to choose things off the menu that people love to eat.

Never, ever go for that strange menu item that has never been ordered. There is a good chance that the ingredients will be old, and that means additional levels of bacteria. A safer bet would be to bank on a nice toasted sandwich, a pizza, or a burger.

Again, I would strongly advise avoiding pasta and other heavily-sauced options. Bars are not known for their high-quality food. Food, in fact, is often perceived as secondary to the "party vibe" that a bar wants to put out into the world.

This is not always the case, and I have had some incredible meals at bars. As an avid bar explorer, remember that what you see in the front is better than what you see in the back. If the bar is filthy, then the kitchen is going to be similar.

You want to target stock rotation, commonly ordered foods, and nothing with fish in it. The bar would have to be something special for me to trust it with seafood, which is hard enough to handle correctly to avoid food poisoning.

Chat to the waiter or barman about their favorite dish, but also keep the upselling angle in mind. Foods combined with popular drinks could be great as well, and they will be among the best sellers in the bar. Along with the seafood issue, I would avoid chicken altogether. Bad chicken in a moist, warm, bacteria-ridden bar is going to land you in the hospital.

If you stick to the bestselling dishes and focus on clean flavors, you should be able to get away with food that tastes good or at the very least cannot be passed off as fresh. Salads should also be left out of the equation as these are generally not washed correctly, are prepared by hand, and are slathered with a salad dressing to hide any slimy leaves.

Better Drink Options

You have arrived at the world's dingiest, most suspicious bar. You need to order a drink! The safest bet for you is to avoid anything that comes out of a tap. The draft beer pipes can be moldy, are never cleaned out, and can contain huge colonies of bacteria. If you have ever tasted a weirdly-flavored draft beer, it probably came from a dirty pipe!

Resist the temptation to order a fancy artisan cocktail at a bar where beer is the most common thing ordered. The same can be said for other types of bars. If you are in a martini bar or a bar where rum is the focal point, do not order wine! It may be old and primed to give you a very bad evening.

There are many reasons why you should opt for something in a bottle, like a beer or cider. The ice in that dingy bar could be really bad, and the straws could have cockroach eggs in them. You just do not know until you are down for the count, retching your lungs out.

If you are going to order a drink on ice, make sure there is no residual taste from bad liquor or bad ice by avoiding sweet mixers. These tend to mask the flavor, and you will be drunk before you realize you have consumed something dangerous or foul.

Vodka, whiskey, brandy, and gin are all easily identifiable drinks with distinct flavors. You should know by drinking these neat if there is anything wrong with them. If you cannot stomach them neat, order a shot of lime on the side, then add it after you have tasted the alcohol in your glass.

Alternatively, anything bottled and sealed is a good play. If you enjoy wine, order it by the bottle instead of the glass. Make sure that the waiter opens the bottle next to you and does not come to your table with an open bottle. This could have been diluted or mixed or may not be the original alcohol in there. It is rare, but it does happen.

Many food writers[57] decide to order bottled beer if they find themselves in a dodgy place. This is because many bartenders can make a bad tasting drink, and you never know why that is. It could be due to flat soda, or it could be due to cheaper alcohol. If you want total safety, my recommendation is always to bet on a sealed bottle.

---

57 *What Drink Do You Order at a Bad Bar? 25 Food Writers Share Their Safety Drinks, http://www.thekitchn.com/food-writers-safety-drinks-170951*

CHAPTER 11

DO NOT DRINK THESE DRINKS!

> *"I would consider myself a regular at my favorite bar, but there's nothing normal about me."*
>
> JAROD KINTZ

If you are a regular at a bar, then you will know your local spot better than I do. This is for the adventurous souls among us that like to strike out and experience new things. Every bar is different; there are outside bars, inside bars, and traveling bars.

They all face their own unique set of challenges. Volume and hygiene are always a concern, and because of that, I have come up with a list of a few drinks and drink accompaniments that you may want to avoid. This is how you drink in relative safety.

The Beer on Tap Conundrum

Did you know that beer on tap can give you violent food poisoning? I did not know until it happened to me. I asked the tap cleaning guy from a major supplier all about this. I see him at a lot of restaurants and know him by name.

The funny thing is I only see him. I never see anyone else—no one at all. I have often wondered if they might have had conflicting schedules that kept a second man from my sight for 14 years. As it turns out, his company was the only one doing it.

Where are all the other suppliers? It makes you think! I have talked him into or have bribed him with food or cash to clean the competitors' taps more than once. He told me that food poisoning is more than possible with a dirty tap. Unclean lines and salt water can quickly turn a nonchalant draft beer into a mini atomic bomb of bacteria.

You have to know if the lines are kept clean[58] by the bar owner if you are a lover of draft beer. Many craft beer places rely on their beer, so you can bet they have a tap cleaner. But privately-owned bars that do not will eventually end up poisoning their customers.

The first signs of an unclean tap are headaches after just one beer. These days I limit my exposure of draft beer to a pint or two on St, Patrick's Day, when the lines are flowing.

Sweet Mixers & Drinks

Cockroaches[59] and other disgusting bugs of all shapes and sizes absolutely love sugar. If you can give it to them in syrup form, even better! In every bar across the United States, you will find a selection of sweet mixers for your spirit-alcohol drinkers.

These sweet mixers are like magnets for all manner of pests, which is why bars can sometimes have the worst roach and pest problems of them all. I once heard a rumor that grenadine and other sweet mixers' coloring comes from crushed up insect guts.

---

58 Kendall Jones, The Elephant in the Room: Dirty Draft Beer Lines, http://www. washingtonbeerblog.com/elephant-room-dirty-draft-beer-lines/

59 6 Foods That Attract Cockroaches, http://www.pest-control.com.sg/blog/6-foods-that-attract-cockroaches.html

While I am confident that this is not true, what is true is that there is a very good chance your grenadine has had many insects crawling over and inside it during its lifetime. It is impossible to keep these mixers capped because they always have pourers on them. This makes them prime targets for fruit flies, roaches, and beetles.

There are some really great tasting aperitifs I enjoy, and I still get an impulse to have one every now and then, but I resist it as best I can. Unless I'm sure it is a quick seller, I will save these drinks for home consumption.

All sticky, syrupy liquors attract bugs! A bug might not be the worst thing in the world, but it does carry diseases. And where there are bugs, there are usually rats, the biggest disease carriers of them all. Standing liquors that never sell will become contaminated with insects very quickly. Faster selling mixers will still be all right but never 100%.

For some strange reason, I have never seen an insect in coffee liquor or Irish cream. These are the two magical liquors that they do not seem to like, which is great news.

Pourers and Bar Staff

A pourer is a barman's best friend. They fit on standard bottles and make it possible to put caps aside for easy pouring, hence the convenient name. Pourers are great because they help control the flow of liquor, measuring it out in a continuous stream.

The best bartenders can pour the same amount of liquor into multiple glasses just because they know the weight and feel of the stream. It makes their job easier, which helps the bar make more money. The only problem with pourers, however, is that they rarely come off once they go on. Patrons have to finish the bottle first, and this can take some time.

While your vodkas, brandies, and whiskeys might be used relatively quickly, other alcohols can stand for days, even weeks, waiting to be used at a bar. This does not bode well for these particular beverages, which will become playgrounds for pests and their bacteria.

Bar staff cannot be bothered with pourer hygiene. I have seen it a zillion times! Unfortunately, this means that pourers get dipped more than they get washed, if at all. I have seen pourers go directly into the mouths of patrons then used to pour consecutive drink orders.

Many types of pourers,[60] like the tapered metal pourer and standard metal pourer, are susceptible to fruit fly infestations and other nasty little critters that never stop coming for the sweetness inside the bottles.

It is a great sign if the bar has invested in sealed pourers that make bug infestations impossible, but in my experience, they are rare. You are more likely to find them at the high-end hotel bars than at your average bar in town. Most of the time bar owners buy the all plastic pourer, which is cheap and a bug favorite.

At this point, I do not need to go into high detail about the germs and disease that flow into your glass when these pourers are used. They are among the most disgusting of all bar implements and items, including the ice machine.

Straws & Swizzle Sticks

Just when you think a bar cannot get more horrifically foul, in walks that companion of drinks everywhere—the straw. Traditionally, straws have been thought to be more hygienic than placing your lips on an unclean glass and ingesting the germs that way.

We have used straws in the modern world for 120 years, and they have helped people keep their lips away from contact bacteria. If only they were completely problem free. The straw, however, is not free of its own set of problems.

---

60 *Everything You Never Wanted to Know About Pourers, http:// thetruthaboutbartending.com/2012/09/04/everything-you-never-wanted-to-know-about-pourers/*

Many bars leave straws[61] out for anyone to take, and these are always the first things people grab when they are looking for something to play with. Your servers and bartenders even play with the straws on slow days. Straws are nearly always contaminated with human bacteria, and I have seen some disturbing sights.

Straws are also notorious hiding places for bug and roach eggs, where they are protected from the outside world. A bar that has a pest problem is likely to have these eggs in their straws, especially if they are stored by the sweet mixers!

Swizzle sticks have the same exact problem—they are fun to play with and end up being touched by multiple people and used in imaginative ways. When customers have access to straws and swizzle sticks, you have to assume that they are filthy.

There are some straws, however, that are individually wrapped, which is far more hygienic. Choose to use the wrapped straws if you are given a choice. If there is no choice, perhaps a rinse would help the straw. If you suspect the glasses may be dirtier, risk it. If the glasses look clean, leave the public straw alone.

The Ice Revelation

How many times have you seen someone order a Scotch on the rocks in the movies and thought, "That looks great." Enough to prompt your own investigation of the drink yourself, I am sure. Drinking spirits on ice has been around forever. The ice cools the room temperature liquor down and gives it a crisp flavor.

I believe I have said enough about ice cubes to put you off ice for the rest of your life. But I added this little section in here for a very important reason. If you think that restaurant ice machines are bad, wait until you learn what happens after it leaves the machine!

First, there is the scoop and ice buckets, which may or may not be regularly washed or properly stored. From there, it travels to

---

61 *Do You Want Germs With That Milkshake?*, *https://germguy.wordpress. com/2010/07/05/do-you-want-some-germs-with-that-milkshake/*

some sort of bin, which is even more likely to be rarely cleaned. If you are unfortunate enough to find an older bar well sink with the heavy, awkward cooling plate, it will most likely have a collection of slime and other dirt beneath it. There is another scoop in this bin. Does this one get cleaned? Maybe.

Often customers sit right above this ice bin while eating, talking, smoking, wadding up their napkins, and shooting baskets. In addition to the various paper and other items found from the customer you will often find beers, wine, and personal staff drink containers that are opened, drank from, and restored in the ice. If this is not enough, you may occasionally find bugs, lizards, broken glass, screws, and spilt beverages in there.

Lastly, we can watch out for the rare but thoughtless bartender re-dipping used cups and using his hands as the scooper.

The next time you feel like a Scotch on the rocks, look around first. You may want to hold those rocks. Buy a bottled water that has been in the fridge (not in a pitcher), and use that to cool your drink instead. It is not as cold, but it will be many times as clean.

Signs of a Hygienic Restaurant

CHAPTER 12
BEST PRACTICES FOR CUSTOMERS

> *"Safety is something that happens between your ears, not something you hold in your hands."*
>
> JEFF COOPER

I have told you everything I know about the gross, dirty, and disgusting things that happen in the restaurant industry. No industry is perfect, and hospitality involves a lot of people, which means a lot of germs and problems.

In this final chapter, I will walk you through some best practices so that you can identify and spot a clean restaurant to maximize your chance of finding one that has great hygiene, food, and service-based practices. It takes a team to make a restaurant experience amazing!

Assessing the Location

Every restaurant deserves the benefit of the doubt at least once before you make a judgment call. I have been to some dodgy places and had the most amazing experience, and I have been to some obviously impeccable places and had terrible experiences.

The goal of this six-step process is to be able to assess the experience[62] that you have when you first visit your chosen restaurant. At any time during your experience, you can get up and leave. Writing down your assessment will make choosing in the future a breeze.

STEP 1: Assess your location.

- What part of town is the restaurant in?
- Is this area known for good food, great restaurants, and excellent service?
- Does the area have a pest problem?
- Does the location provide for all of your needs?
- Is the restaurant area and the outside parking lot safe?
- Is the area known for drinking, fights, and other mishaps?

WARNING SIGNS

- ✗ A poor location with an ill-kept shopfront
- ✗ The absence of other customers
- ✗ An outdated and musty appearance
- ✗ A restaurant that looks and smells bad

---

62   *What Do Customers Look For in a Restaurant Experience?*, *http://www. lightspeedpos.com/blog/2015/04/what-do-customers-look-for-in-a-restaurant-experience/*

Assessing the Staff

The next step in the process is to take a hard look at the staff and assess them based on three general categories: mood, technical ability, and presentation. Staff should generally be welcoming, smiling, and happy to see a guest arrive at their door.

They will be fully competent[63] at their jobs, not making too many mistakes along the way. They will also look neat and professional. Wrap this up with a helpful tone, and you have a recipe for a darn good waiter.

I have met many servers over the years, and I have been one many times. I know what a tough job it is. But all great servers try their best throughout the day. They take things seriously and bend over backwards to make their customers happy.

STEP 2: Assess the staff.
- Do the staff appear to be happy with their jobs?
- Do the staff present themselves professionally and with a clean uniform?
- Do the staff make you feel welcome?
- Do the staff take all the pressure out of the dining experience?
- Are the staff helpful?
- Can you grab anyone and ask them a question?
- Are the questions answered logically, or do they seem like lies?

---

63 *Ruth Mayhew, How to Assess Staff Competency, http://smallbusiness.chron.com/assess-staff-competency-49404.html*

WARNING SIGNS
- ✗ Staff that look exhausted and overworked
- ✗ Staff that look dirty and disillusioned
- ✗ Staff that are not happy to be there
- ✗ Staff that do not want to help you for any reason
- ✗ Staff that purposefully lie to get sales
- ✗ Staff that seem disorganized, preoccupied, or disinterested in their business

Assessing the Food & Drinks

Once you have been invited inside the restaurant and shown to your seats by the lovely staff, you will get a chance to scan the menu and experience[64] the main reason you are there—the food! Assessing food and drinks should work according to the problems I have raised in this book.

You will want to avoid the major pitfalls or take a pre-emptive strike before being poisoned! Do this by smelling and looking at your food. Make sure it smells appealing and fresh. Check that the salad and extras are also fresh—because it matters.

Focus on eating slowly in case there is anything that has been cooked into your food. I once found a rusty nail in a stew I ordered from a local bistro! Ask yourself these questions, and give an honest rating for each out of five.

---

64 *Bharath M. Josiam, Assessing Quality of Food, Service and Customer Experience at a Restaurant: The Case of a Student Run Restaurant in the USA, http://www. researchgate.net/publication/263927162_Assessing_quality_of_food_service_and_ customer_experience_at_a_restaurant_the_case_of_a_student_run_restaurant_in_the_ USA*

STEP 3: Assess the food.

- Is the menu logical, fresh, and comprehensive?
- Does the menu cater for all tastes?
- Did you get what you ordered off the menu?
- Was the food presented well?
- Was the food visually appealing?
- Was your food hot when it arrived?
- Did the food taste fresh?
- Was the food delicious?
- How long did the food take to get to your table?
- Was your drink in a clean glass?
- Did the ice seem fresh?
- Did your drink taste good?

WARNING SIGNS

- ✘ Old, slimy accompaniments like wilted salad on your plate
- ✘ Ice cubes that taste funny
- ✘ An aroma from your plate that is not appealing
- ✘ Everything looks grey like it was cooked in old oil
- ✘ Everything smells the same
- ✘ Food that is lukewarm or extremely cold

Assessing the Service

When you find a new restaurant, a large portion of your experience will depend on the level of service that you get there. In fact, a major part of what you are paying for is the service quality. That is why it matters how well the staff perform, how quick they are to respond to your needs, and how well they are able to meet them.

A waiter's skill[65] has a lot to do with the service quality. An excellent waiter will be able to balance being friendly with being professional, and they will not make obvious mistakes. They also have the ability to deal with mistakes better, which puts the customer at ease.

There is nothing worse than a flustered, overworked waiter that cannot manage to execute a simple order because they are in such a panic. In ruins the experience for everyone involved. Good waiters can get through a busy service and make everyone happy that they came out for a meal.

STEP 4: Assess the service.
- What is the waiter's greeting skill like?
- Does the team look organized and ready to help?
- Did anyone else offer you assistance during your experience?
- Did the waiter take your order well?
- Did the waiter answer your questions clearly and honestly?
- Did the waiter establish a comfortable relationship with you?
- Did the waiter bring your food on time?
- Did the waiter bring you what you ordered?
- Did the waiter clear the plates at the right time?
- Did the waiter check on your needs?
- Did the waiter bring you your bill on time?
- Did you feel hurried to leave or welcome to stay?

---

65 Sara Dickerman, Table Manners, http://www.slate.com/articles/life/food/2007/09/table_manners.html

WARNING SIGNS

- ✖ A harassed temperament in your waiter
- ✖ Distraction and boredom in your waiter's voice
- ✖ Any kind of attitude that is not friendly or helpful
- ✖ Messing up your order and not apologizing for it
- ✖ Getting things wrong consecutively
- ✖ Making you feel hurried for table turnover
- ✖ Waiting around for your waiter to show up
- ✖ Feeling neglected and forgotten
- ✖ The waiter not caring about your problems
- ✖ The waiter not wanting to help you

Assessing the Popularity

Restaurants are all about other people and the vibe they bring to the setting. A restaurant might have all the ingredients to be great, but the people irritate you. This can happen due to drinks specials, the fact that it gets too loud, or too many people are packed into a small space. Popularity is about going to a restaurant more than once.

You need to take multiple people to this restaurant to see if it is consistent and a great place to take friends and family. If the place in question has passed your four previous steps, then you are happy to return there. The only thing that is left for you to do is to invite others to come with you and see what they think!

STEP 5: Assess the popularity.
- What are the people like that go to the restaurant?
- Is it a fun place to enjoy a dinner?
- What kind of fun is it?
- Did your friends enjoy it?
- What did they like or not like about the place?
- Were there lots of people each time you went?
- Did you go at different times/days?
- Are people talking about this new restaurant?
- Do you feel like you love hanging out there?

WARNING SIGNS
- ✗ The inability to chat to friends because the music is blaring
- ✗ A restaurant that attracts rude people or heavy drinkers
- ✗ A restaurant that is far too cramped
- ✗ A restaurant where the bathroom is always busy
- ✗ A restaurant where everyone is too busy for the little things

Assessing and Review

The very last thing that you need to do is write a restaurant review. You would have used them at the beginning of your restaurant search to help you decide where to go. Now you need to add to the global knowledge of the place and publish your opinion.

A good restaurant review is earned by a number of hardworking staff and a talented business owner. They really do work tirelessly night after night to make a new place successful. A restaurant does not have to be "happening" to be perfect.

But it does need to be clean and fun, with great food and good people. Those are the building blocks of having an incredible restaurant experience. Anything less and people need to know about it. You would want to when you first checked on the reviews.

STEP 6: Assess and review.
- Take all of your experience, and write it down.
- What was the place like?
- What were the people like?
- Was the food good?
- What made it a restaurant worth visiting?
- What gave it that little something special?
- Was the service excellent?
- Were the prices in line and competitive?
- Tell your story to others.

Then once you have created your perfect review,[66] publish it on TripAdvisor or Yelp. Each time you do this you leave an account for yourself and for others. Soon you will find that within a year you have explored many places deeply and passionately.

Now that you understand the secrets of the restaurant industry, your reviews will be even more useful to the novice restaurant hunter that only wants to find a great experience.

---

66   *David Farkas, How to Write Like a Restaurant Critic: Tips on How to Make Your Online Dining Reviews Stand Out From the Yelp, Urban Spoon Babble, http://www. cleveland.com/dining/index.ssf/2014/02/how_to_write_like_a_restaurant.html*

Conclusion

I am pleased to say that your ride through this book is complete! You have raced through the pages, learning all about the ins and outs of the torrid world of food service and hospitality in the USA. No one knows more about the secrets of service now than you do!

Restaurants want your business, and I want to be part of the movement that helps good people find good experiences. Now that you have been filled in on how restaurants really work (and what their dirty little secrets are), you will be in a better position to make judgments about a place.

For many years, I wondered whether people knew the disgusting and often disturbing things that went on behind the scenes with people and their food. Let us all try to be better. At the end of the day, we all want to go to a nice restaurant and have a good time.

Even the people that work in the restaurant industry are customers at other establishments. Together we can make it a stronger, healthier experience for everyone. The onus is on you, the consumer, to understand how to protect yourself against unscrupulous restaurateurs.

From the world's dirtiest ice machines, to pests nibbling at your salad goods, to rude servers and burnt out managers, I hope this trusty book has given you some insight into what it takes to run a darn good restaurant. Because it takes a lot—and deserves the fame it gets from customers willing to stop and post a kind review.

Now get out there into the restaurant world and experience the food, fables, and foibles for yourself. You are the only one who can decide whether that place will become a family favorite. Just get online and find something that appeals to you in your area.

Better, safer experiences start now!

Carrie Herring

References

Chapter 1

Restaurant Quotes, http://www.brainyquote.com/quotes/keywords/restaurant.html

Peters, David, S, *Top 5 Mistakes Of Mom And Pop Restaurants,* http://therestaurantexpert.com/top-5-mistakes-of-mom-and-pop-restaurants/

Mom And Pop, http://www.investopedia.com/terms/m/momandpop.asp

Strauss, Karsten, *13 Mistakes New Franchises Make – And How To Avoid Them,* http://www.forbes.com/sites/karstenstrauss/2014/05/27/13-mistakes-new-franchisees-make-and-how-to-avoid-them/

Davis, Amy, *Restaurant Report Card: Country Club Has Hygiene Issue,* http://www.click2houston.com/news/money/restaurant-report-card-country-club-has-hygiene-issue/28020056

Mistakes To Avoid When Running Your Bar, http://www.entrepreneur.com/article/232499

Aleccia, JoNel, *Caterers Dish Up More Cases Of Food Poisoning,* http://www.nbcnews.com/id/38420815/ns/health-food_safety/t/caterers-dish-more-cases-food-poisoning/#.VX_zuvmqpBc

Chapter 2

Restaurant Quotes – Page 2, http://www.brainyquote.com/quotes/keywords/restaurant_2.html

Mc Cullen, Ashlee, *Epic Restaurant Pranks,* http://www.johnnaknowsgoodfood.com/2012/04/25/epic-restaurant-pranks/

Kurtz, Annalyn, *Subway Leads Fast Food Industry In Underpaying Workers,* http://money.cnn.com/2014/05/01/news/economy/subway-labor-violations/

Bourdain, Anthony, *Things To Avoid When Eating In Restaurants,* http://www.theguardian.com/books/2000/aug/12/features.weekend1

Ashe-Edmonds, Sam, *What Do You Do When You Have A Short Staff In The Kitchen,* http://yourbusiness.azcentral.com/short-staff-kitchen-10544.html

Geier, Kathleen, *Why Are Working Conditions For Restaurant Employees So Bad?* http://www.washingtonmonthly.com/political-animal-a/2013_03/why_are_working_conditions_for043617.php

Chapter 3

Funny And Fun Quotations About Restaurants, Food, Waiters And Dining Out, http://retailindustry.about.com/od/usretailsalescalendar/a/Funny_inspiring_famous_quotable_quotations_restaurants-dining-eating-out-waiters-food.htm

Elizabeth, C, *How To Review A Restaurant Like A Pro,* http://thedish.restaurant.com/how-to-review-a-restaurant-like-a-pro/

Cleanliness: The Restaurant Table, http://directorslounge.hubpages.com/hub/Cleanliness-The-Restaurant-Table

Golwert, Lindsay, *7 Germiest Places; Germs Lurk On Menus, Lemon Wedges, Condiment And Soap Dispensers,* http://www.nydailynews.com/life-style/health/7-germiest-places-germs-lurk-menus-lemon-wedges-condiment-soap-dispensers-article-1.469626

Schocker, Laura, *This Will Make You Never, Ever Want To Put A Lemon Wedge In Your Water Again,* http://www.huffingtonpost.com/2014/01/27/lemon-germs-wedges-restaurants_n_4659168.html

Gentile, Dan, *Things You Have To Explain To People Who've Never Worked In Kitchens,* http://www.thrillist.com/eat/nation/understanding-cooks-best-kitchen-advice

Chapter 4

Insect Quotes, http://www.brainyquote.com/quotes/keywords/insects.html

A Bug's Love Affair With Food, http://www.mybugproblem.com/blog/a-bugs-love-affair-with-food-benton-pest-control

Menon, Anil, Dr, *Pest Management In Restaurants,* http://pestcontrol.basf.us/news-&-events/feature-stories/archive/pest-management-in-restaurants.pdf

Pests Share Hot Spots & Solutions, http://facilitymanagement.com/articles/maintenance-2013-06-4.html

Food Pests Love, http://www.holderspestsolutions.com/blog/post/foods-pests-love

Cockroach Food, http://www.orkin.com/cockroaches/cockroach-food/

Rosario, Frank, Algar, Selim, *Half Of Upper East Side Restaurants Are Rat-Infested: Study,* http://nypost.com/2014/02/18/half-of-upper-east-side-restaurants-are-rat-infested-study/

Chapter 5

Employees Quotes, http://www.brainyquote.com/quotes/keywords/employees.html

Sietsema, Robert, *Why I hate Upselling In Restaurants, And The Emergence Of Narrative Upselling,* http://www.villagevoice.com/restaurants/why-i-hate-upselling-in-restaurants-and-the-emergence-of-narrative-upselling-6555268

Burks, Frances, *The Effects Of Bad Hiring In A Restaurant,* http://smallbusiness.chron.com/effects-bad-hiring-restaurant-36458.html

Bouchez, Colette, *Food Allergies: Tips For Eating Out,* http://www.webmd.com/allergies/features/food-allergies-tips-for-eating-out

Jong, Tracy, *Obstacles For Restaurant Uniforms,* http://tracyjonglawfirm.com/rwlblog/?p=240

Morran, Chris, *Study: Gloves No Substitute For Hand-Washing When It Comes To Food Prep,* http://consumerist.com/2010/10/13/study-gloves-no-substitute-for-hand-washing-when-it-comes-to-food-prep/

Mc Querrey, Lisa, *How To Confront Employees With Disturbing Habits,* http://smallbusiness.chron.com/confront-employees-disturbing-habits-44193.html

Chapter 6

Customer Quotes, http://www.brainyquote.com/quotes/keywords/customer.html

Walsh, Matt, *Maybe You Get Bad Customer Service Because You're A Bad Customer,* http://www.huffingtonpost.com/matt-walsh/bad-customer-service_b_3799574.html

Customers Behaving Badly: How To Avoid Being One Of Them, http://tiethemoneyknot.com/customers-behaving-badly-how-to-avoid-being-one-of-them/

Maguire, Patrick, *64 Suggestions For Restaurant Customers,* http://www.servernotservant.com/2009/11/05/64-suggestions-for-restaurant-customers/

Potter, Caroline, *Diners Behaving Badly: What Annoys You About Other Restaurant Patrons,* http://blog.opentable.com/2010/diners-behaving-badly-what-annoys-you-about-other-restaurant-patrons/

Waiters And Waitresses Reveal The Worst Things A Customer Can Do, http://magazine.foxnews.com/at-home/waiters-and-waitresses-reveal-worst-things-customer-can-do

Chenetz, Ruth, *What Would You Do? Rude Customers Insults Server,* http://abcnews.go.com/WhatWouldYouDo/rude-customer-insults-server/story?id=12638062

Chapter 7

Dirt Quotes, http://www.brainyquote.com/quotes/keywords/dirt.html

Merwin, Hugh, *Another Study Determines Restaurant Ice Machines Contain More Bacteria Than Toilet Water,* http://www.grubstreet.com/2013/06/ice-machines-bacteria-toilet-water.html

Levine, Beth, *The Germ-Filled Truth About Restaurants,* http://www.grandparents.com/health-and-wellbeing/health/food-borne-illnesses

Does A Killer Live Inside Your Dirty Ice Machine? http://tekexpressny.com/dirty-ice#.VZpj0vmqpBc

Van Luling, Todd, *3 Gross Things You Didn't Know Were In Your Ice Cubes,* http://www.huffingtonpost.com/2014/06/16/ice-cubes-gross_n_5475301.html

Dirty Ice Makers Will Get You Sick, http://www.newair.com/articles/dirty-ice-makers-will-get-you-sick/

Neumann, Karl, MD, *Hold The Ice: Germs Survive Freezing, Alcohol,* http://articles.chicagotribune.com/1989-08-13/travel/8901040291_1_ice-cubes-drink-bacterial-count

Chapter 8

Sales Quotes, http://www.brainyquote.com/quotes/keywords/sales.html

The 5 Secrets Restaurants Don't Want You To Know, http://www.doctoroz.com/article/5-secrets-restaurants-dont-want-you-know

Blahd, William, *Food Poisoning,* http://www.webmd.com/food-recipes/food-poisoning/food-poisoning

Restaurant Hazards Posed By Commercial Fryers, http://www.foodservicewarehouse.com/education/product-safety-public-health/restaurant-hazards-posed-by-commercial-fryers/c28213.aspx

Abelson, Jenn, Daley, Beth, *On The Menu, But Not On Your Plate,* http://www.boston.com/business/articles/2011/10/23/on_the_menu_but_not_on_your_plate/

Tuder, Stefanie, *10 Things Restaurants Won't Tell You,* http://abcnews.go.com/blogs/lifestyle/2013/12/10-things-restaurants-wont-tell-you/

A Former Maître d' Explains Why You Should Stay At Home On Valentine's Day, http://www.thekitchn.com/a-former-maitred-explains-why-you-should-stay-home-on-valentines-215854

4 Reasons To Avoid The "All You Can Eat" Buffet, http://www.thealternativedaily.com/4-reasons-avoid-can-eat-buffet/

Chapter 9

An, Jenny, *Top 20 Drinking Quotes Of All Time*, http://philly.
thedrinknation.com/articles/read/11386-Top-20-Drinking-Quotes-of-
All-Time#

Meltzer, Matt, *The Oldest Bar In Every State (And DC)*, http://www.
thrillist.com/travel/nation/america-s-oldest-bars-the-oldest-bar-in-all-
50-us-states-and-washington-dc

Easthope, Andrew, *Coffee Machine Cleaning Tips*, http://www.
fivesenses.com.au/blog/2013/11/05/coffee-machine-cleaning-tips

Duron, Alexandra, *How Restaurants Can Make You Sick, Bad Food
Has Nothing To Do With It*, http://www.prevention.com/health/healthy-
living/restaurant-silverware-can-cause-illness

Cox, Ted, *Problem Bars Could Be Closed By Top Cop Under Proposed
New Ordinance*, http://www.dnainfo.com/chicago/20150323/downtown/
problem-bars-could-be-closed-by-top-cop-under-proposed-new-
ordinance

Buchtmann, Lydia, *Fact Buster: Can You Smell If Food Is
Off?* http://www.abc.net.au/health/talkinghealth/factbuster/
stories/2014/12/11/4146849.htm

Chapter 10

Famous Quotes About Drinks, http://www.barbarossa.com.au/famous-
quotes-drinks/

Perrone, Marielaina, *Share: The Dirty Dozen – Dirtiest Items We Place
In Our Mouths*, http://www.empowher.com/community/share/dirty-
dozen-dirtiest-items-we-place-our-mouths

Don't Fruit The Beer, http://bartenderdiary.blogspot.com/2010/07/dont-
fruit-beer.html

What Is The Danger Of Counterfeit Alcohol? http://www.flask.com/
what-is-the-danger-of-counterfeit-alcohol/#.VZmFfmqpBc

Double-Dipping – Explain It To Me. http://chowhound.how.com/
topics/768856

Chapter 11

Quotes by Jarod Kintz http://www.goodreads.com/author/quotes/4157885.Jarod_Kintz

Jones, Kendall, *The Elephant In The Room: Dirty Draft Beer Lines,* http://www.washingtonbeerblog.com/elephant-room-dirty-draft-beer-lines/

6 Foods That Attract Cockroaches, http://www.pest-control.com.sg/blog/6-foods-that-attract-cockroaches.html

The Truth About Bartending: Everything You Never Wanted To Know About Bartending, http://thetruthaboutbartending.com/2012/09/04/everything-you-never-wanted-to-know-about-pourers/

Beer Pong Games Carry Risk Of Salmonella, e.Coli And Staph Germs, Research Finds, http://www.nydailynews.com/life-style/health/beer-pong-games-carry-risk-salmonella-e-coli-germs-article-1.1317048

Do You Want Germs With That Milkshake? https://germguy.wordpress.com/2010/07/05/do-you-want-some-germs-with-that-milkshake/

Chapter 12

Safety Quotes, http://www.brainyquote.com/quotes/keywords/safety.html

What Do Customers Look For In A Restaurant Experience? http://www.lightspeedpos.com/blog/2015/04/what-do-customers-look-for-in-a-restaurant-experience/

Mayhew, Ruth, *How To Assess Staff Competency,* http://smallbusiness.chron.com/assess-staff-competency-49404.html

Josiam, Bharath, M, *Assessing Quality Of Food, Service And Customer Experience At A Restaurant: The Case Of A Student Run Restaurant In The USA,* http://www.researchgate.net/publication/263927162_Assessing_quality_of_food_service_and_customer_experience_at_a_restaurant_the_case_of_a_student_run_restaurant_in_the_USA

Dickerman, Sara, *Table Manners,* http://www.slate.com/articles/life/food/2007/09/table_manners.html

Farkas, David, *How To Write Like A Restaurant Critic: Tips On How To Make Your Online Dining Reviews Stand Out From The Yelp, Urban Spoon Babble,* http://www.cleveland.com/dining/index.ssf/2014/02/how_to_write_like_a_restaurant.html

About the Author

Carrie Herring is a career waitress/bartender but has also been a hostess, cooked, and sold produce door to restaurant door. She has a plethora of experience in the food and beverage industry. She has worked in very small, family-owned diners where she was the only employee as well as a large casino with well over ten thousand employees. Country clubs, rum bars, tourist traps, corner bar, corporate chains, brand new first-time newbie eateries, and failing restaurants—Carrie has seen it all. To round it all off, her months as a delivery/salesperson gave her access to dozens of other kitchens. Church kitchens, veterans' halls, and other private clubs where she spent her youth also round off her experience.

Made in the USA
Lexington, KY
29 September 2015